# REMEMBER THE ALAMO!

## The Battle for Texas Independence

MOVEMENTS and MOMENTS THAT CHANGED AMERICA

# REMEMBER THE ALAMO!

## The Battle for Texas Independence

Karen Clemens Warrick

ROSEN PUBLISHING

Published in 2021 by The Rosen Publishing Group, Inc.
29 East 21st Street, New York, NY 10010



**Library of Congress Cataloging-in-Publication Data**

Names: Warrick, Karen Clemens, author.
Title: Remember the Alamo! : the battle for Texas independence / Karen Clemens Warrick.
Description: New York, NY : Rosen Publishing, 2021. | Series: Movements and moments that changed America | Includes bibliographical references and index. | Audience: Grades 6-12.
Identifiers: LCCN 2019013432 | ISBN 9781725342156 (library bound) | ISBN 9781725342149 (pbk.)
Subjects: LCSH: Alamo (San Antonio, Tex.)--Siege, 1836--Juvenile literature. | Texas--History--Revolution, 1835-1836--Juvenile literature.
Classification: LCC F390 .W337 2021 | DDC 976.4/03--dc23
LC record available at https://lccn.loc.gov/2019013432

Portions of this book originally appeared in *Alamo: Victory or Death on the Texas Frontier.*

**Photo Credits:** Cover, p. 3 North Wind Picture Archives/Alamy Stock Photo; pp. 6–7 Steven Frame/Shutterstock.com; p. 11 Everett Historical/Shutterstock.com; pp. 12–13, 22–23, 37, 39, 85 Bettmann/Getty Images; p. 17 GraphicaArtis/Archive Photos/Getty Images; pp. 18, 29, 32, 33, 78–79 Library of Congress Prints and Photographs Division; p. 21 Print Collector/Hulton Archive/Getty Images; p. 25 Interim Archives/Archive Photos/Getty Images; p. 43 Copyright © North Wind Picture Archives; p. 47 Fine Art/Corbis Historical/Getty Images; p. 53 Jim Cole, Photographer/Alamy Stock Photo; p. 56 Business Wire/Getty Images; p. 60 Billy Hathorn/Wikimedia Commons/File: Juan Seguin grave and monument, Seguin, TX IMG 8164.jpg/CC BY-SA 3.0; p. 65 The Picture Art Collection/Alamy Stock Photo; p. 67 Larry D. Moore/Wikimedia Commons/File: James Bonham Texas Centennial Statue.jpg/CC BY-SA 4.0; p. 74 Stock Montage/Archive Photos/Getty Images; p. 76 Ed Vebell/Archive Photos/Getty Images; p. 87 FLHC 76/Alamy Stock Photo; p. 93 Pumbaa80/Wikimedia Commons/File: Flag of the Republic of Texas (1836–1839).svg/Public Domain; pp. 96–97 Universal Images Group/Getty Images; pp. 98–99 Niday Picture Library/Alamy Stock Photo; p. 104 Maksym Kapliuk/Shutterstock.com (flag), Justin Toney/Shutterstock.com (Texas longhorn), Jim and Lynne Weber/Shutterstock.com (monarch butterfly), Leena Robinson/Shutterstock.com (Texas bluebonnets); pp. 106–107 Sunset Boulevard/Corbis Historical/Getty Images; pp. 108–109 MicheleB/Shutterstock.com; pp. 112–113 Robert Alexander/Archive Photos/Getty Images; cover and interior pages banner graphic stockish/Shutterstock.com.

CPSIA Compliance Information: Batch #BSR20. For further information contact Rosen Publishing, New York, New York at 1-800-237-9932.

# CONTENTS

# INTRODUCTION

The Texas Convention of 1836 met at Washington-on-the-Brazos on March 1. Delegates gathered in an unfinished building. There were no doors. Windows were covered by cotton cloth. The unheated room was chilled by a freezing north wind. "Everyone [was] shivering and exclaiming against the cold," noted an observer, but spirits were high.[1] After a call to order, officers were elected. A committee was selected and quickly went to work.

As delegates worked, reports arrived from the Alamo. Santa Anna had surrounded Texians, or early settlers of the Texas Territory, defending the old mission only days before, on February 23. Delegates wanted to go to their defense, but they had a more important mission at hand. It was time to declare independence from Mexico. The next day, the committee presented its draft. Following are portions of the original text:

> [The Mexican] government has ceased to protect the lives, liberty and property of the people

**The Alamo is an enduring symbol of the Texas fight for independence of the 1830s. It remains today a landmark and testament to Texians' perseverance. Visitors can tour the building and remember its past.**

> ... a statement of our grievances is therefore submitted to an impartial world, in justification of the hazardous but unavoidable step now taken, of severing our political connection with the Mexican people and assuming an independent attitude among the nations of the earth.

> The Mexican government ... invited ... the Anglo-American population of Texas to colonize the wilderness under ... a written constitution, that they could enjoy the constitutional liberty and republican government to which they had been habituated in the land of their birth, the United States of America.
>
> In this expectation they have been cruelly disappointed ... changes made in the government by General Antonio Lopez de Santa Anna, who overturning the constitution of his country, now offers us the cruel alternative either to abandon our homes ... or submit to the most intolerable of all tyranny.
>
> It [the government] has invaded our country both by sea and by land, with intent to lay waste our territory, and drive us from our homes; and has now a large ... army advancing, to carry on against us a war of extermination.
>
> ... Grievances, were patiently borne by the people of Texas, until they reached that point at which forbearance ceases to be a virtue. We then took up arms in defense of the national constitution ... The necessity of self-preservation, therefore, now decrees our eternal political separation ...[2]

On March 2, 1836, the people of Texas declared independence. The vote by fifty-nine delegates was unanimous.

Now delegates could focus on the Texians defending the Alamo. They were relieved when news arrived that three hundred fifty reinforcements led by James Fannin were marching toward the Alamo. The latest letter from

Lieutenant Colonel William Travis, dated February 25, reported that a Mexican attack had been fought off. It seemed the Alamo was secure. To celebrate independence, Texas delegates went on a two-day drinking spree—eggnog fortified with spirits.[3]

If the news had reached the Alamo defenders, they would have celebrated, too. They had been battling for independence since Santa Anna surrounded the mission. Now it was official.

1

# SANTA ANNA

In February 1836, weeks before Texians declared independence, General Santa Anna and his troops were marching north. Their target was San Antonio de Béxar. Santa Anna planned a surprise attack on the Texian soldiers there, and the plan almost worked. Soldiers in Béxar had celebrated George Washington's birthday the night before. The party continued until sunrise. Many were going to bed when a messenger rode into town and sounded the alarm. The Mexican cavalry was waiting for orders to attack. They were only 8 miles (13 kilometers) away on the banks of Leon Creek. Santa Anna planned to crush the Texas uprising. The Texas Territory belonged to Mexico.

The villagers were alarmed by the news. María de Jesús Olivarri dug a hole in the clay floor of her house. She buried the family savings. Then she loaded a two-wheel oxcart and set out for the family ranch. She took along her six-year-old son, José, and his cousin, Pablo. People all over town prepared to leave. They piled clothing, bedding, pots, and pans into carts. Many walked away from San Antonio, carrying only what they could. Their children hurried along behind them. No one wanted to be caught in the middle of the battle between General Santa Anna and the rebels.

Antonio López de Santa Anna, better known as General Santa Anna, led the Mexican army during the Battle of the Alamo.

## Sound the Bell

Lieutenant Colonel William Travis was one of the co-commanders of the Texian troops in San Antonio. A messenger delivered the warning about General Santa Anna. Travis and Dr. John Sutherland hurried to the San Fernando Church. The two men ordered a guard to follow them as they climbed the winding stairs up the tower. They looked to the south and then to the west for any signs of the Mexican army. All they saw were the trees, bushes, and winter grass that covered the rolling prairies.

The men were relieved. The messenger's information seemed to be false. Just to be safe, Travis ordered the guard to keep watch. If he saw anything suspicious, he was to ring the church bell.

Travis went back to work in his office. Sutherland stopped to visit with Nat Lewis, who owned a store on Main Plaza. Sutherland and Lewis passed the next couple of hours taking inventory, counting spools of thread, pots, plates, and other goods.

Suddenly, the bell clanged. Sutherland and Travis raced to the church. When the guard saw them, he called down from the tower, "The enemy is in view!"[1] Both men raced up the stairs to make sure the guard's report was true. They looked out the tower window. Again they saw nothing.

It seemed to be another false alarm. The sentry defended himself. He said he had seen hundreds of mounted Mexican cavalry a moment before. They had turned off the road into a grove of mesquite trees out of view.

Travis sent Sutherland to scout the territory. John Smith, a soldier who knew the area well, went with him. They worked out a simple signal before they left. If the two men

**This illustration shows Lieutenant Colonel William Travis (right) watching troops head out to battle at the Alamo in 1836.**

found nothing, they would walk their horses back to town. If they discovered signs of the Mexican army, they would return at a hard gallop.

Sutherland and Smith rode south and climbed a hill. They were alarmed by the sight they saw from the top.[2] The guard was right. Santa Anna's cavalry was less than 2 miles (3 km) from San Antonio. Sutherland scanned the troops, taking a quick count. He thought about fifteen hundred horsemen were ready to attack.

The two men turned and galloped for town. Before they had gone far, Sutherland's horse slipped in some mud. The scout was thrown from the saddle. His horse fell across his legs, injuring his hip. Smith raced back and helped Sutherland into his saddle. Meanwhile, the sentry in the church tower had spotted their hasty retreat. He rang the bell, sounding the alarm.

## Taking Cover in the Mission

Mexican troops were closing in on the Texas rebels. Travis ordered his troops to take cover inside the Alamo. Once an old Spanish mission, it now served as a fort. Its walls offered the best defensive position in the town of San Antonio.

Captain Almercon Dickinson leaped on his horse. He pulled his wife, Susanna, and their baby, Angelina, up behind him. They galloped across the San Antonio River and all reached the Alamo safely.

Others also hurried to the mission. Ana Esparza came with her four children. Petra Gonzales was a very old woman. She could not walk away from the village. Several African American slaves also hurried to the fort. There were more than a dozen women and children. No one knows exactly how many. No list was made of all their names.

## William Travis at the Alamo

At the outbreak of the Texas Revolution, William Travis was commissioned as an officer in the Cavalry Corp. He arrived at the Alamo on February 3, 1836, and brought forty men with him. He believed Texas should be independent. He was willing to fight to the death. Travis was a capable commander and brave soldier when it counted. He held the Alamo defenders together. He did everything possible to defend the San Antonio de Béxar. His last messages showed he planned to stay and fight, though he would likely lose. He also seemed to understand that if the Alamo fell, the men inside would become martyrs in the battle for Texas independence.

Travis and James Bowie shared command of the Texas troops. Bowie made sure his two sisters-in-law reached the Alamo safely. Then, he led a band of soldiers to search the town. The men herded any cattle they could find into the fort's corral. They hauled in sacks of grain. They also grabbed any guns they found. They would need these supplies and more. The Mexican army was already too close. Bowie expected them to surround the Alamo. Everyone would be trapped inside, but there was no safer place to make a stand.

As the defenders hurried inside the Alamo, Sergeant William B. Ward waited at the main gate. He was looking after the guns that protected the entrance. Ward often drank too much alcohol, but this day he was sober.[3] His guns were ready to fire at the Mexican army.

When the gates closed, fewer than two hundred defenders were inside the Alamo's walls. Even with the odds stacked against them, the Texas rebels prepared to fight. They would not surrender to General Santa Anna.

## Send Aid Soon

Before the enemy arrived, Travis sent messengers for help. Jim Bonham went to Goliad. The town was about 95 miles (153 km) away. The message asked Colonel James Fannin and his men to march immediately. The defenders of San Antonio needed the three hundred fifty Texas troops under Fannin's command.

Travis also sent the injured scout, Sutherland, for help. He galloped 60 miles (97 km) east to the town of Gonzales. The ride was painful. His injured hip made it difficult to sit on his horse. When Sutherland arrived at Gonzales, he asked for volunteers to return with him to the Alamo.

David "Davy" Crockett had arrived in San Antonio a few days earlier. He was ready to help, too. Travis sent Crockett to guard the palisade, or wall. It ran from the southeastern corner of the mission to the chapel. Crockett's men were sharpshooters. They were the best defenders inside the walls of the Alamo. With their long rifles, they could hit targets up to 200 yards (183 meters) away.

## Surrounded

As soon as everyone was inside the mission, the gates were pulled closed. Less than thirty minutes later, the Mexican army swarmed into San Antonio. A small band paraded into the Main Plaza. They played marching tunes as more troops arrived. Standard bearers came first. They carried the battle flags of Mexico. The cavalry and infantry followed.

## Davy Crockett

David "Davy" Crockett was born in Tennessee on August 17, 1786. Crockett was an excellent shot. He often took part in shooting contests and almost always won. He was also a natural leader. He represented Tennessee in Congress from 1827 to 1833. In 1835, he ran again and was defeated. He was not used to losing. He is reported to have said, "You may all go to Hell and I will go to Texas."[4] He left Tennessee in November 1835. He rode into San Antonio and soon signed on to fight for independence. During the Battle of the Alamo, Crockett often showed himself to the enemy. He dared them to take aim and fire. Today, folktales remember him as the "king of the wild frontier," and stories about him are still told.

Davy Crockett is often imagined as a man who wore deerskin clothing and carried a gun, as this portrait shows.

**The San Fernando Cathedral was an important part of the Battle of the Alamo. It is there that Santa Anna's soldiers hung their flag that told their opponents to surrender or face the deadly consequences.**

Santa Anna's soldiers climbed the stairs of the San Fernando Church tower. It was about 800 yards (732 m) outside the walls of the Alamo. The soldiers unfurled a blood-red flag. They hung it high for everyone to see. It was a message. General Santa Anna was telling the Texas rebels that there would be "no quarter—no mercy—surrender must be unconditional."[5]

The townspeople who had not left prayed they could stay out of the way. They knew a vicious battle was about to begin.

2

# SPAIN CLAIMS MEXICO

In 1518, Hernán Cortés set sail from Cuba. He was commander of a Spanish expedition sent to explore new lands to the west. When his fleet reached land, Cortés and his men set to work building a settlement near today's city of Veracruz, Mexico. Cortés was soon ready to explore more of the new land. He marched inland in search of riches. His expedition captured lands occupied by the Aztecs and claimed the territory for Spain. Mexico City, the capital of New Spain, was built on the ruins of the Aztec capital, Tenochtitlán.

Texas was a part of New Spain. The territory was located far north of the capital. At first, the Spaniards ignored the area. Then, in the late 1600s, France showed interest in it.[1] The French claimed lands that bordered Texas. French settlers wanted to move west. Spaniards wanted to protect their claim. They needed more citizens to live in Texas. It was time to encourage settlers to move to the territory.

## Hernán Cortés

Hernán Cortés was born in Spain in 1485. He led the Spanish conquest of the Aztec Empire in 1519. It took three months to reach the Aztec capital city. His troops had to fight their way through dense jungle terrain.

Montezuma II was the leader of the Aztecs. Cortés's arrival coincided with an Aztec prophecy. The natives expected the arrival of a white-skinned god from the East. Montezuma II initially welcomed Cortés and gave him many gifts. The two leaders' relationship soon deteriorated. Fearing that the Aztecs would attack, Cortés took Montezuma II hostage. A battle followed. Montezuma II was struck by a stone and killed. The Spanish were driven from the city, but Cortés did not give up. He gathered his forces and returned to the Aztec capital. The city fell after a three-month siege by the Spanish forces.

## Religion and Guns

The Spaniards had a plan. It was one that had worked in the past. They sent missionaries to New Spain. Their job was to convert the native people to Christianity. They also taught them to follow Spanish laws. Soldiers came with the priests. The soldiers were to protect the missionaries from unfriendly natives. Spanish missions and forts sprang up across Texas Territory.

This painting shows Spanish conquistador Hernán Cortés (left) meeting the Aztec leader Montezuma II (right).

One mission and fort was built on the San Antonio River. Settlers came to the area and a small town grew. It was called San Antonio de Béxar. In 1714, a chapel was built. However, the priests had little success converting natives to Christianity. The people in the region were Apache and Comanche. These native peoples did not want to become Spanish subjects. Their warriors attacked settlers who tried to live in the area.

By the early 1800s, little had changed in the region. Few Spaniards from Mexico settled in Texas. The important cities of New Spain were too far away. Fewer than five thousand people called Texas home. About half of them lived in San Antonio.

## Americans Welcome

In 1803, the United States bought land from France. The land was known as the Louisiana Purchase. Louisiana was a huge territory and it greatly expanded the borders of the United States. The territory stretched from New

From the 1500s to the 1800s, Spanish missionaries arrived in New Spain and Texas. They built churches and houses, and tried to make the native people believe in Christianity.

Orleans all the way to Canada. Many Americans wanted to move to the area of the Louisiana Purchase and farther south, including Texas. They were eager to move west.

Moses Austin, originally from Virginia, wanted to help US families move west. He wanted them to settle in Texas. In about 1820, he went to San Antonio de Béxar. He spoke to the town leaders, offering to bring settlers to the territory. At first, his offer was turned down. Then the Spaniards thought it over. They needed more people to settle in Texas. Maybe Austin's colony was the answer to their problem.

The Spaniards told Austin he could start his colony. They granted him two hundred thousand acres in Texas. Three hundred families could settle on the land. Unfortunately, Austin did not get to carry through with his plan. He died in 1821. That same year, Mexicans won their independence from Spain.

## A Mexican Territory

By 1824, Mexico encouraged settlers from other countries to move to Texas. Settlers had to agree to become Mexican citizens. They had to join the Catholic Church. However, they did not have to pay taxes for the first ten years they lived in the Texas Territory. This gave families time to get on their feet before they had to support Mexico.[2]

Stephen F. Austin was the son of Moses Austin. After his father's death, Stephen took charge of his father's land in Texas. He brought settlers to an area near the Brazos River. They set up the colony of San Felipe. Land sold for twelve-and-a-half cents an acre. It was cheap and there was plenty for everyone.

Soon, many US settlers lived in Texas. More than sixteen thousand called it home. These families built houses, farms,

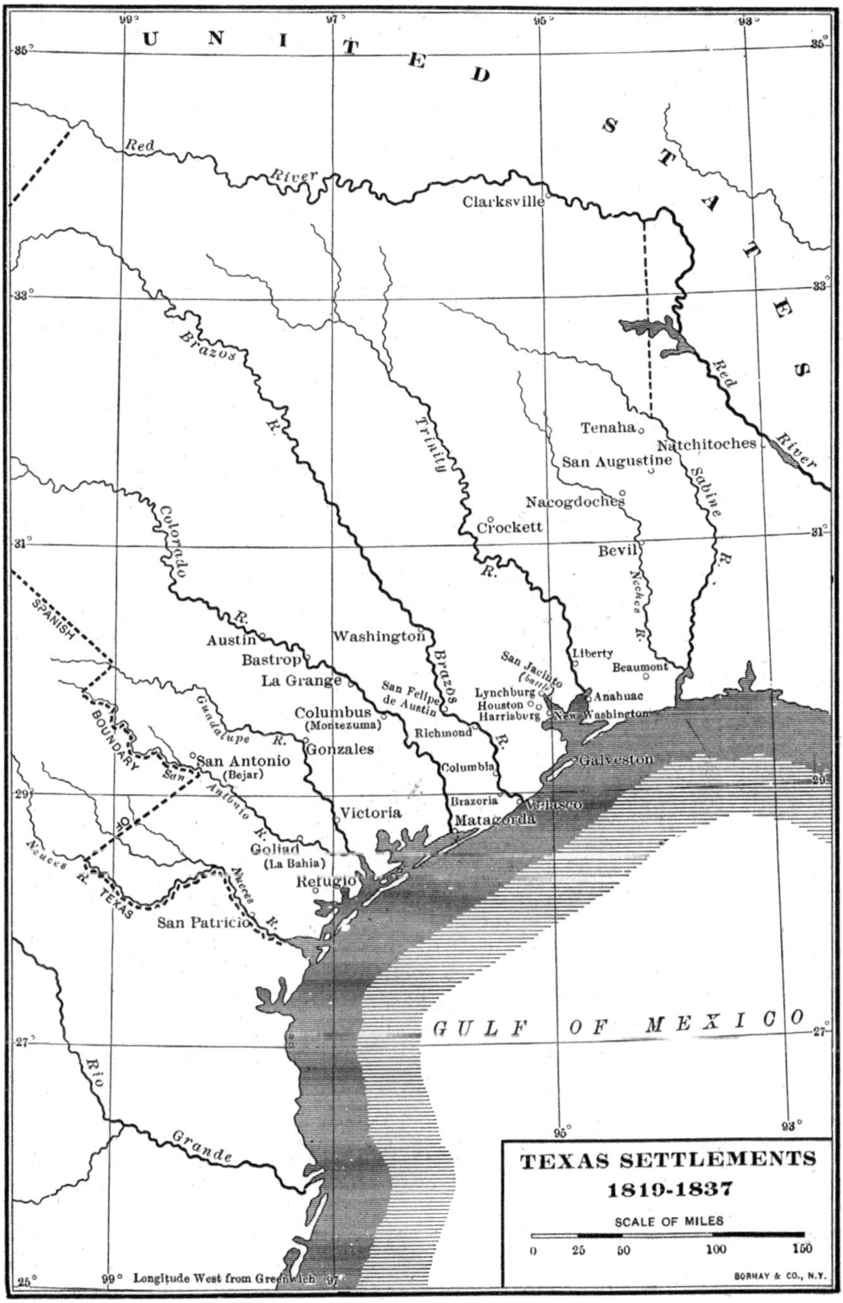


This map shows where different people settled in Texas between 1819 and 1837.

and ranches. Their little villages sprang up across Texas. Names like Columbia, Brazoria, and Gonzales were added to the map of Mexico.

Texas settlers had a tough life. Their homes were crude log cabins. Floors were made of wood planks. Windows had no glass. The settlers sat on homemade stools and ate from plank tables. Gourds were used to dip water and to serve food. Clothes were made of buckskin or homespun wool. Goods shipped into Texas were very expensive. Most of the settlers could not afford to pay the high prices.

Danger lurked everywhere. One night, a woman in Gonzales barely escaped from a wildcat. It pounced from the dark shadows, killing her dog. Native tribes were also a threat. They stole horses and raided crops. They tried to drive the settlers out.

Life was especially hard for female settlers. It was their job to pound corn into meal and to prepare food. They had to spin cotton to make and mend the clothes. Women also made soap, molded candles, and took care of the children. There was great truth in the words of one pioneer that Texas was "heaven for men and dogs—but hell for women and oxen."[3]

But settlers had reasons to stay in Texas. There was plenty of land. They had neighbors that could help them. Best of all, the Mexican government paid little attention to those living in the territory.

## New Rules for Texas

Mexico's plan to settle Texas had worked. In fact, it worked better than expected. Many had moved to Texas. After six years, immigrants from the United States outnumbered people born in Texas. US immigrants made up 75 percent of the population in Texas.

Now the Mexican government had new problems. Large parts of Texas lands were owned by Americans. Many had entered the territory illegally. They did not obey Mexican laws. They smuggled goods into the region. These American settlers often refused to join the Catholic Church.

In 1824, the Mexican government adopted a new constitution. It gave states many rights. But Texas was no longer a separate territory. Settlers were part of a new state called Coahuila y Texas. Coahuila was a mining area. Texas had many farms and ranches. More people lived in Coahuila; people in Texas were outnumbered five to one. Laws passed by the new state government usually helped miners in Coahuila, not the farmers and ranchers in Texas.

The US government offered to buy Texas, but Mexico would not sell it. Mexican officials were worried that the United States would try to claim the territory anyway. In April 1830, Mexico passed a new law. This law allowed settlers to come from countries in Europe. Limits were placed on settlers from the United States.

By 1831, Mexican troops were stationed all over Texas to keep any more settlers out of the territory. The central government tightened its control. States and territories lost many of their rights.

American settlers in Texas were outraged.[4] They wanted to run their own territory. They also wanted Texas to be a separate Mexican state. To earn statehood in Mexico, eighty thousand people needed to live in Texas. Less than half that number lived in the region in 1831.

The American settlers began to call themselves Texians. They protested changes they did not like. Two political

## Stephen Austin and Texas

Stephen F. Austin worked for the Territory of Texas. He helped US citizens settle in Texas.

He raised a militia, or army of local people, to protect settlers from Native American raids. This was the first police force in Texas. Later, it became known as the Texas Rangers.

At first, Austin was a good Mexican citizen. He followed the laws of the country. He served in the legislature. He had many American and Texian friends in the territory. When trouble developed between the state and the Mexican central government, Austin joined the Peace Party. He opposed those who wanted Texas to break away from Mexico.

After Austin was thrown in jail, he realized he could no longer be loyal to the country of Mexico. He could not support Santa Anna. Austin now believed it was time for all Texans to stand for independence.[5]

parties formed: the Peace Party and the War Party. Stephen Austin was a member of the Peace Party. It was loyal to the Mexican government. Many settlers joined the War Party. These Texians believed Texas needed to be independent from Mexico. William Travis was a member of that group.

This painting, called *The Settlement of Austin's Colony*, shows Stephen Austin (center) encouraging troops to fight Native Americans in Texas. A scout stands at the door, ready to give a message. The painting hangs in the Texas state capitol building.

## The State of Texas

In January 1833, Mexican voters elected General Santa Anna the new president of their country. At first, Texians were pleased. Santa Anna had helped write the Constitution of 1824. They thought he would help Texas become a separate state. They believed he would give them back the right to rule their own territory.

But the Texians were disappointed. So they and Tejanos, or Mexican-born citizens living in Texas, took action. They sent delegates to a meeting in San Felipe. Stephen Austin attended the meeting. This committee wrote a state constitution for Texas.

The delegates asked Austin to take their proposed constitution to Santa Anna in Mexico City. He agreed to go, but Santa Anna was away when Austin arrived in the capital. Instead, Austin met with Valentín Gómez Farías, the acting president. Austin presented Texas's request for statehood. It was rejected. Now Austin was angry. He wrote a letter to Tejano friends in the Texas territory. He suggested that it was time for Texas to break away from Coahuila. His letter did not reach his friends. Instead, someone took it to Gómez Farías. He had Austin thrown in jail.

While Austin was in jail, Santa Anna canceled the Constitution of 1824. Troops were sent to the Texas Territory. They closed down the legislature. Delegates were arrested. The customs house was reopened. Settlers were ordered to pay taxes. By 1835, Santa Anna ruled Mexico as a dictator. The general sent troops north, intending to drive all Americans from Mexico.

3

# MEXICO GOES TO WAR

Domingo Ugartechea was the commander of Mexican troops in San Antonio. He had orders to take back a cannon from Texians in the town of Gonzales. He sent a soldier to collect the cannon, but he returned empty handed, reporting that the Americans of Gonzales refused to surrender their weapon.

Ugartechea knew how high tensions were between the Texians and Santa Anna's government. It would be easy to spark hostilities. General Martín Perfecto de Cos sent about one hundred soldiers to Gonzales to take the cannon. He ordered them to use force only if necessary. Cos wanted to avoid conflict. The company rode out of San Antonio de Béxar on September 27, 1835.

The settlers still refused to hand over the cannon. The Mexicans claimed they needed it to defend San Antonio. The townspeople were sure that was not the real reason. They knew Santa Anna planned to disarm them. Taking the cannon was the first step. They needed it, they said, to defend their town from Native American attacks.

**This cannon was buried in a peach orchard and then resurrected before Mexican forces as they approached the city of Gonzales. It is now on display at the Gonzales Memorial Museum.**

They buried the cannon in a peach orchard near town. One hundred forty men prepared to defend their prize. Cos had not been ordered to attack and decided to wait for reinforcements. Meanwhile, the people of Gonzales prepared a surprise.

## "Come and Take it"

On October 2, 1835, Mexican troops gathered on one side of the Guadalupe River. The men of Gonzales waited on the other side. They stood around the cannon. It had been dug up and mounted on wagon wheels. A banner flew over it.

The large flag was decorated with a picture of the cannon and the words "COME AND TAKE IT."

Before sunrise, the Texians crossed the river. Fifty men on horseback went first. They were followed by the cannon with its flag. Men on foot marched after them. There were almost three hundred citizens in the group.

The Texians tried to surprise the Mexican army, but a barking dog alerted a guard. It was dark and foggy. No one could see what they were shooting at. The Texians sat down and waited for daylight. When the sun came up, they were in a field of corn and watermelons. The Mexican army was about 300 yards (274 m) away.

This banner honors the flag that flew over Gonzales on October 2, 1835.

The Texians loaded the cannon and fired. It was the first shot of the revolution.

The settlers charged the enemy lines. The Mexican troops returned fire briefly. Then, their commander ordered them to retreat to San Antonio. Newspaper reports compared the skirmish at Gonzales to the first battle of the American Revolution at Lexington, Massachusetts. Gonzales became known as the "Lexington of Texas." It is remembered for being the first battle of the Texas War for Independence.[1]

## Texas Declares War

On October 4, Austin told the San Felipe committee, "War is declared." It was time to "drive the [Centralist] Military out of Texas."[2] Texas volunteers grabbed their weapons and flocked to Gonzales. Austin was elected the commander-in-chief of the Army of the People. Other officers were Colonel James Bowie, Colonel James W. Fannin, and Colonel William B. Travis.

On October 11, Austin issued his first order. The army would leave the following day for San Antonio, where General Cos waited with most of his troops. A week later, the Army of the People was camped by the San Antonio River. They were within sight of the old Alamo Mission. The first clash occurred at the end of October. Cos sent about three hundred soldiers to drive the rebels away. Ninety Texians took cover along the riverbanks. They hid behind trees and fired at the enemy. After several attempts, the Mexican troops were forced to retreat. They left behind sixteen dead and one cannon. During the next month, Cos tried to drive the Texians off without success. Austin tried to take the town, but he failed. So far the Battle for San Antonio was a tie.

On November 24, Austin got new orders. He was to go to the United States to rally support for the war. Austin turned over his command to General Edward Burleson.

Burleson ordered an attack on San Antonio. Several officers refused to obey him. By December 4, 1835, Burleson decided he had only one option. He had to pull back.

Another officer, Benjamin Milam, disagreed with the withdrawal. He thought the time was right to attack. Milam voiced his opinion to other volunteers. Then, he drew a line across the ground and yelled, "Who will go with old Ben Milam into San Antonio?"[3]

Three hundred soldiers took his challenge. For the next few days, the Texians attacked. They fought their way into San Antonio. They moved forward street by street. They took cover behind fences and houses. Their sharp shooting forced the Mexican troops to retreat. Cos withdrew across the San Antonio River to the Alamo Mission. More Mexican troops arrived on December 8. They still could not stop the Texas rebels. Early the next morning, Cos surrendered. Texians now controlled San Antonio. They had driven the Mexican military from their land.

## Benjamin Milam

Ben Milam believed in Texas independence. He fought with a company of soldiers commanded by George Collinsworth and helped capture Goliad.

Milam played a role in the battle for San Antonio. Three hundred volunteered after Milam made his famous plea: "Who will go with old Ben Milam into San Antonio?" The attack began at dawn on December 5. The battle ended on December 9, with the surrender of Cos and the Mexican army.

Milam died on the third day of the battle for San Antonio. He was shot in the head by a Mexican sniper. Milan was a hero of the Texas Revolution. He was buried just a few steps from where he fell. His grave was in the courtyard of a house in the town.

## Taking Command

The Texas Territory was at war. Immediate action was needed. The rebels had to form a government. Many committee members had joined the Army of the People. They had to be called back to San Felipe. Finally, enough members had returned by November 3. Now the committee could set to work.

The committee elected Henry Smith as governor. A general council was created to help Smith. Sam Houston was appointed major general of the armies of Texas. He

## Sam Houston

Before the Texas war for independence, Sam Houston was an important figure in United States and Native American negotiations. He grew up among a Cherokee tribe and was even adopted as an official member, taking on the name of Black Raven. However, in 1817, he was involved in the removal of Cherokee from Tennessee to land in Arkansas, which was then a US territory. His reputation eventually led him to politics and got him assigned to an office in Texas in 1832. It was there he became involved in Texas's fight for freedom from Mexico and truly made history.

Following independence, Houston was elected Texas's first president. The town of Houston was the republic's capital. The city of Houston, Texas, was founded in 1836 and named in his honor.

This painting shows Sam Houston riding a horse in San Jacinto, a Texas city. It is on display at the San Jacinto Museum.

had a tough job. He was given the task of putting together a more organized army. This was difficult at first because many soldiers in the Army of the People were loyal to their own leaders and did not want to adapt to a new system.

## Texians Take a Stand

Houston sent Colonel James Bowie to San Antonio. On January 19, 1836, he rode into San Antonio with thirty soldiers. He met with Colonel James C. Neill, who had been left in charge of the town.

Bowie looked around the town. It had been built on the inside of a bend in the San Antonio River. Two plazas formed the town center. The San Fernando Church sat on the west side of one plaza. Many of the town's most important citizens lived nearby. By 1836, about two thousand people lived in San Antonio.

Bowie had orders from Houston to destroy the Alamo. Neill and his Texians were to pull back to Gonzales. However, the building had its benefits.

Before taking action, the two officers toured the Alamo compound. There was a large rectangular-shaped courtyard in the center. It was 154 yards (141 m) long and 54 yards (49 m) wide. Stone walls 3 to 4 feet (0.9 to 1.2 m) wide and 9 to 12 feet (3 to 4 m) high surrounded the courtyard. On the north and west sides, small adobe rooms lined the wall. A long one-story building known as the long barracks ran along the south wall. The main entrance, a 10-foot-wide (3-meter-wide) passageway, was near this building.

There was a gap on the southeast of the courtyard where the chapel had been built. It sat 50 yards (46 m) away from the long barracks. General Cos had built a low wall of dirt and timber across the open space.

This drawing shows what Colonel James Bowie looked like.

Neill and Bowie also knew the Alamo stood in an important location. It blocked one of two major roads leading into Texas from the south. Likewise, an artilleryman, Neill observed that the Alamo had more cannons than any other fort west of the Mississippi River. However, the number of troops stationed at the Alamo could not defend it easily. Neill and Bowie estimated that it would take almost one thousand soldiers to defend the old mission. At that time, Neill had eighty men. Bowie only had thirty. Even if they had the numbers necessary, they had no money to pay that many soldiers. There were no funds to buy food or clothing for them either.

On February 3, their numbers grew slightly after Colonel Travis arrived, bringing thirty more volunteers with him. That was still far fewer than desired.

Neill and Bowie understood all these problems, and yet due to the advantages of the Alamo, they decided not to leave San Antonio. Even before Travis's arrival, on February 2, Jim Bowie sent Governor Smith this message about the Texians' decision: "Colonel Neill and myself have come to the solemn resolution [decision] that we will rather die in these ditches than give it [the Alamo] up to the enemy."[4] They did not destroy the mission. They believed the future of Texas depended upon taking a stand right there.[5]

4

# LESSON FOR THE TEXIANS

Santa Anna could not respond immediately to the Texian uprising. Some Mexican politicians feared a military takeover and had reduced the size of the regular army.

Santa Anna needed to recruit and train a new army. He had left Mexico City and moved north to organize his forces. Many of his men had little or no experience. They learned to march in formation and load and fire muskets quickly. Training continued for most of the month of January. Santa Anna also trained his soldiers to recognize bugle calls. One bugle call made Santa Anna's intentions clear. It was the signal to give "no quarter" or mercy to the enemy. Anyone standing against Santa Anna and his army would be killed.

Santa Anna disliked the Texians. In his eyes, they were squatters who lived illegally in Mexican territory. Many claimed large pieces of land. Jim Bowie was one example. He held more than seven hundred thousand acres. These Texians did not practice the Catholic religion. They smuggled in goods. They kept slaves. They paid no attention to the laws of Mexico.

Santa Anna was spurred into action after the Battle of San Antonio. The Texians thought they had won. Santa Anna was ready to prove them wrong.

## Surprise Attack

In January 1836, the commander-in-chief gathered his forces. He handled every detail himself. Money was needed to buy supplies for his army. He collected funds from the church. He took out loans in his own name.

Santa Anna gave orders to his generals. They were to collect 100,000 pounds (45,360 kilograms) of hardtack. The hard pieces of bread would be used to feed the army. The cavalry needed five hundred horses. Supplies were loaded on two- and four-wheeled carts pulled by mules and oxen.

Next, Santa Anna had his generals train four thousand new recruits. Many were Mayan natives who lived in Southern Mexico. They spoke no Spanish but quickly learned to follow orders. They had no choice. It was either learn to fight or be killed on the spot. Santa Anna planned to mix new recruits with experienced brigades and cavalry units. This would create a strong army—one that could drive all the rebels from the Texas Territory.

By February 1, 1836, he was ready. The general sent one final report to the Secretary of War and Navy: "[A]lready the whole army is marching for the Capital of San Antonio de Béxar whose plaza I will occupy precisely before the end of the month. Today it begins, despite the fact that the distance from here is almost 600 miles [966 km]."[1]

Then Santa Anna joined his army and marched toward the Alamo. He had one goal: he would regain control of the Texas Territory for Mexico.

**General Santa Anna leads soldiers. He is dressed in a lively uniform with bright red and yellow colors.**

Santa Anna decided to surprise the Texians guarding the Alamo. Winter weather made travel difficult. They would not expect him to attack before spring.

On January 25, 1836, Santa Anna watched his troops on parade. Officers were dressed in dark blue uniforms with red fronts. The cavalry rode lively horses. The soldiers' swords and lances gleamed in the sun. Four thousand foot soldiers marched. They wore blue cotton uniforms and homemade sandals. On their heads were tall black hats with visors and plumes. All was ready. The commander-in-chief gave orders to march. The Mexican army headed north. The target was San Antonio, a little town held by the Texians.

## The President and Commander-in-Chief

At age forty-two, Antonio López de Santa Anna was a dictator. No one dared question how he ruled his country and commanded the army.

While his soldiers drilled, Santa Anna planned his next move. He would march north quickly. He gave his men little or no time to sleep. The tactic would allow him to surprise his enemy, the Texians holding the Alamo.

Santa Anna was an experienced fighter. He joined the Spanish army at age fifteen and fought Mexican natives in the Texas Territory. His commanders took no prisoners. Mexican rebels were put to death. Some historians believe he learned from their example.

Each day took the Mexican army deeper into the desert. The uneven ground made walking difficult. The troops raised clouds of dust as they tramped along. The dust made it hard to breathe.

By the time they reached the Texas border, the steady march had worn down the troops. San Antonio was still 100 miles (161 km) farther north. The weather created problems. A winter storm blew in. Temperatures dropped. Cold winds kicked up sand and dust. Heavy rain made it hard to see. Cavalry riders could not find their way through mesquite thickets. Snow fell. Conditions were so bad that one hundred oxen died in two days. The foot soldiers huddled together to try and stay warm. Their cotton uniforms offered little protection. Most soldiers did not have tents. The Mayans had always lived in the tropics where the weather was warm. Many died from the bitter cold. Even with all these problems, Santa Anna continued to push his troops north.

The weather warmed, but that caused other problems. The water supply dried up. Without enough to drink, many animals died. The troops were thirsty and worn out. There was not enough food to keep up their energy. The sun left their skin burned and blistered. Some men got sick but kept on marching. Others dropped along the way. They waited to be picked up by one of the wagons or to die along the road.

On February 21, Santa Anna and his army reached the Medina River. They were only 25 miles (40 km) from San Antonio. It was an easy day's ride for the cavalry. Two days later, after a brief rest, Santa Anna moved his troops forward. His surprise was spoiled when the Texians spotted his troops about 6 miles (10 km) from San Antonio. That did not stop Santa Anna. He marched on toward the town.

As the Mexican army approached, a small group appeared at the edge of the village. They raised a flag. It was red, white, and green with two stars in the middle. The stars stood for Texas and Coahuila. It showed them as separate states. These men were probably Mexican-born citizens. They still thought the revolution could be settled peacefully. Santa Anna's army ignored them. The little group lowered their flag and returned to the Alamo.

## Learning from Napoleon Bonaparte

Santa Anna was 5 feet 10 inches (178 centimeters) tall. His eyes and hair were black. He dressed like a prince. He wore a uniform of red and black trimmed with gold braid. A silver and gold sword hung at his side. The sword cost seven thousand dollars.

The general had studied military techniques developed by another dictator and general: Napoleon Bonaparte. The French general divided his forces into smaller units. The units marched several days apart. This made it easier to feed an army on the move.

However, the smaller units were easier to attack and could be defeated before more troops arrived. To solve this problem, Napoleon insisted on better communication. His commanders had to cooperate so that troops could move quickly on and off the battlefield.

## A Shot of Defiance

By three in the afternoon, Mexican troops poured into Military Plaza. Santa Anna was with them. Villagers who had not fled watched the parade. Little Juan Indalecio heard the band. He ran toward the music. He came face-to-face with a tuba. The huge instrument seemed to have a mouth big enough to swallow him. Juan turned and ran home.[2]

Napoleon Bonaparte inspired Santa Anna's military tactics and techniques.

The standard-bearers followed the band. They carried the battle flags of Mexico. One flag stood for the central government. A fierce eagle decorated the banner. The other flag was blood red, indicating that the Mexican army would show no mercy.

Within minutes, the Texians fired the Alamo's 18-pound (8 kg) cannon. The cannon got its name from the size of the cannonballs used. Each one weighed 18 pounds (8 kg). The roar was heard for miles around. Townspeople escaping across the desert looked back toward San Antonio.

The cannon shot showed the rebels' defiance. But there was still hope that the standoff could be settled peacefully. Bowie sent a note asking to parley, or talk, with Santa Anna. At first, the Texian ended his message with a dedication to "God and the Mexican Federation." Then, Bowie changed his mind. He crossed that out and wrote, "God and Texas."[3] A messenger carrying a white flag walked out the gates of the old mission. He slowly approached the Mexican troops.

Santa Anna refused to see the messenger. An aide delivered Santa Anna's answer to the Texians. But he would not discuss terms under any conditions.[4]

By now, Travis knew what Bowie had done and he was angry.[5] They had agreed to make decisions together. Bowie had not talked to Travis before sending someone to talk to Santa Anna. Now Travis decided to send his own man.

The second messenger met with Colonel Juan Almonte. If the Mexicans wanted to talk matters over, Travis would be pleased to parley.

Almonte explained there could be no compromise. He stressed that the Texians' only hope was surrender. They must lay down their arms and promise never to take them up again.

This message was relayed to the Texians inside the Alamo. Travis ordered the cannon fired once more. He later reported in a message to Houston: "I answered them with a cannon shot."[6]

## Under Siege

As evening approached, the Mexican army made camp in San Antonio. Soldiers stacked rifles. They set out mess kits, or gear used to prepare food. They used picks and shovels to build earthworks for their cannon. Colonel Almonte studied the list of captured materiel. Not much on the list was useful.

In the main plaza, Santa Anna dismounted. He handed the reins of his horse to an orderly. Then, he went into a one-story building with a flat roof like most others in San Antonio. This would be his headquarters. The commander immediately began to organize a siege.

Inside the Alamo, Travis and Bowie met and discussed the situation. They sent two more messengers for help. One went to Gonzales. The other went to the fort at Goliad to inform Colonel James Fannin that the Mexican army was in San Antonio. The Texians in the Alamo needed help. Colonel Fannin and his troops must come quickly.

Travis also sent a party out for supplies needed to hold out during a siege. The Mexican force in San Antonio was still small. The rebels could slip in and out of the Alamo under cover of darkness.

Daylight faded. From inside the old mission, the Texians watched the Mexican army settle down in San Antonio. Now, all they could do was wait for help to arrive.

5

# BESIEGED!

At dawn on February 24, the rebels holding the Alamo realized their predicament. They were surrounded by Mexican troops—at least fifteen hundred in number. More were probably on the way. The chances of escape were slim. Women and children sheltered inside the mission walls. Two dozen men were wounded or sick. They could not be moved. The Texians had gathered what provisions they could, but the corn and cattle would last no more than a month. Guns and ammunition were plentiful, but good powder for the cannons was in short supply.

Hope for survival depended on reinforcements coming soon. The defenders believed help would arrive in a few more days. James Fannin and his men were only 95 miles (153 km) away, and Sam Houston was gathering an army of Texians. By the next morning, Travis was now in charge. Jim Bowie could no longer command troops. He had been sick for a week. He had a high fever and was so weak that all he could do was lie in bed.

Two soldiers carried him away to another room. It was along the south wall of the Alamo compound near the main gate. Bowie's final official act was to turn over full command to Colonel Travis.

## Digging In

Travis set his small band of men to work. The walls of the Alamo needed to be stronger. The men dug trenches inside the main plaza. They built structures around the walls to support the cannons. They also dug a well for drinking water and patched a large hole in the north wall with thick logs.

Outside the mission, Mexican troops were also at work. They were just beyond rifle range. They dug a trench and soon had three of their cannons in place. This made work inside the Alamo more difficult. Cannon shells flew over the wall and exploded in the plaza.

Every time a cannon fired, work inside the Alamo stopped. Men like Davy Crockett huddled along the walls. Soldiers crouched on the church roof. Others ducked in ditches outside the wall. Men dodged dirt and stones sent flying by the exploding shells.

In the dark rooms of the church, women and children could not see what was happening. All they could hear again and again were cannons firing at the Alamo.

## Famous Words

The Alamo was surrounded, but messengers still managed to slip in and out of the old mission. For some reason, the Mexicans did not tighten the noose around the Texians. Villagers who had not left San Antonio were allowed to go from the town to the mission. Travis even sent men out to repair damage to the walls.

## A Tall Hero in a Coonskin Hat

When Davy Crocket arrived at the Alamo about the middle of February, people gathered around him in the main plaza. He stepped up on a wooden crate and addressed a cheering crowd. He spoke of the new country of Texas and of patriotism. His speech showed he considered himself one of them. It focused on his support of Texas independence from Mexico: "[F]ellow citizens ... I have come to your country ... to aid you all I can in your noble cause. I shall identify myself with your interests ... and all the honor I desire is ... the liberties of our common country."

"That made many a man who had not known him before Colonel Crockett's friends," Dr. Sutherland remembered.[1]

Crockett lived up to his speech, fighting and dying at the Alamo for Texas independence.

Jim Bonham, the messenger sent to Goliad, returned. He brought news that help was coming. But could it arrive in time? Travis sat down to pen another message. This time he wrote to "The People of Texas & All Americans in the World":

> I am besieged, by a thousand or more of the Mexicans under Santa Anna—I have sustained a continual Bombardment & cannonade for 24 hours & have not lost a man—The enemy has

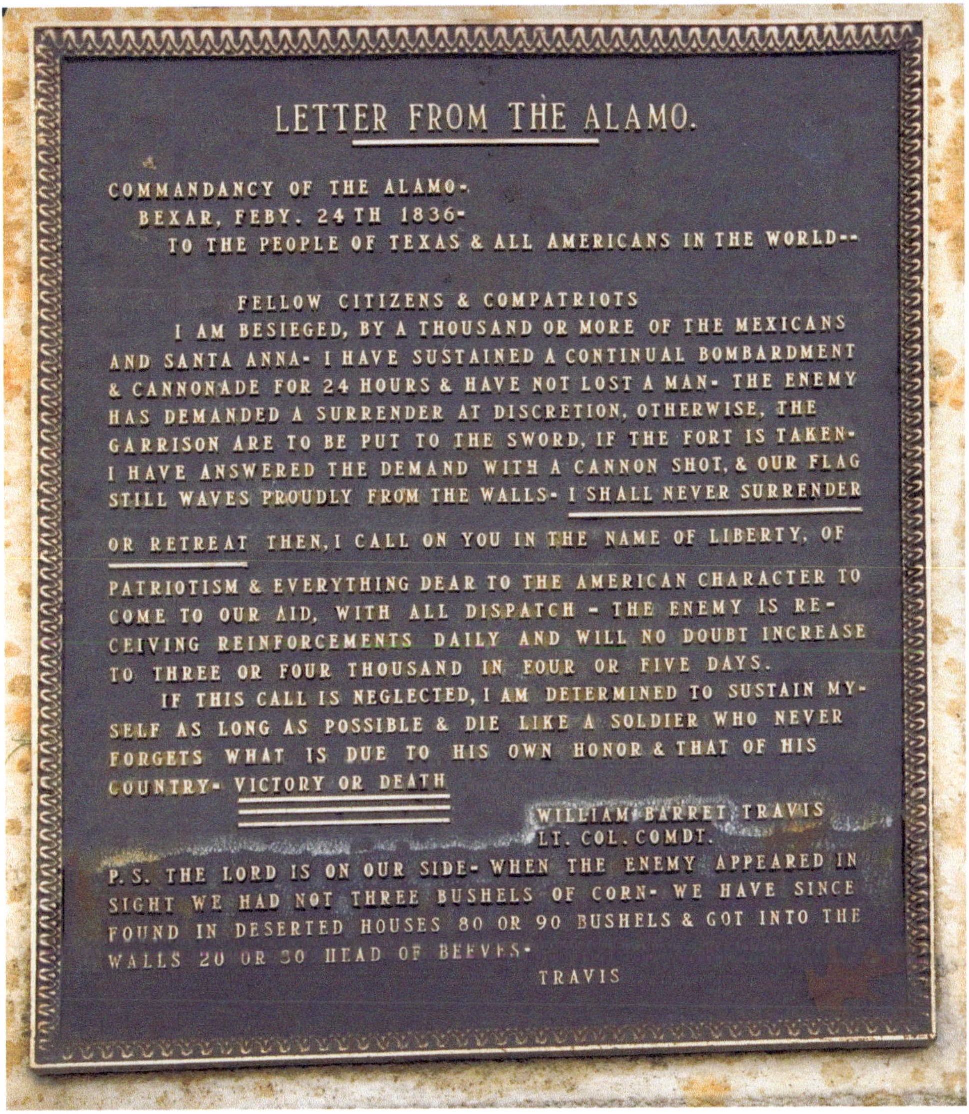


This plaque memorializes Colonel Travis's letter from the Alamo. His words express the difficulties faced and the determination he and his troops had in seeing the fight through to the last man.

> demanded a surrender … otherwise, the garrison are to be put to the sword, if the fort is taken—I have answered the demand with a cannon shot, & our flag still waves proudly from the walls—I shall never surrender or retreat.[2]

Travis went on to ask for immediate aid. Then, he closed the letter with "Victory or Death," followed by his signature.[3]

## Under Fire

By the morning of February 25, 1836, the Mexicans had closed in. They set cannons in place across the river. At ten o'clock, bugles sounded. Two hundred foot soldiers attacked. They fired steadily as they moved toward the walls of the Alamo.

The Texians watched and waited as the enemy swarmed across the river. They held their fire. The Mexicans dodged in and out of huts. These shacks near the mission walls provided cover for the soldiers as they drew closer and closer.

The Texians waited until the enemy was within range. Then, the cannon inside the Alamo roared. The Texians fired with everything they had. They used rifles, muskets, shotguns, cannon, and even pistols. The Mexican line broke under the fierce attack. By noon, they pulled back to the river. They carried at least eight wounded and dead with them. At the end of the skirmish, Travis noted that not one Texian had died. Only two or three men had minor wounds.

The huts that foot soldiers had used as cover were a problem. Travis decided that they had to be burned down. That night, the gates of the Alamo opened. A few men with torches raced toward the nearest shacks. Smoke soon poured from the thatched roofs. The dry wooden walls crackled with flames. The enemy opened fire. However, everyone returned through the gates safely. From inside, they watched as the huts burned to the ground. The job was done.

## A Ride Through the Night

That same night, Travis sent another message. He asked Captain Juan Seguín to find General Houston and ask for immediate help. Seguín had sided with Bowie, Travis, and the other Texians who were fighting against Santa Anna. He had to find a horse to ride before he could set out. His own mount was injured. He went to see Bowie on his sickbed. Bowie agreed to lend his horse to Seguín.

The captain and one other man slipped out of the Alamo under cover of darkness. They rode up the Gonzales road. After a few miles, they came upon Mexican soldiers who had piled up brush to block the road. The soldiers were standing around a fire. They called out to the two riders. Seguín replied in Spanish. The guards thought he was one of their officers. Seguín and his companion rode nearer. When they reached the pile of brush, they spurred their horses, leaping clear. The Mexican soldiers gave chase, but the two men from the Alamo escaped. They delivered the message to General Houston.

## Day Three

The Mexican cavalry attacked the next morning. They rode east, circling around the rear of the Alamo. Texians raced to the wall. They met the attack head on. Rifles blazed, and the Mexicans turned back. Another threat was over.

It was a cold, dreary day. Another storm was moving in. Temperatures dropped. Still, all the men inside the Alamo had many tasks to complete. Some found wood to burn. Others hauled buckets of water from an irrigation ditch. Men dug more trenches. They built up earthworks to strengthen the walls. As they worked, the Mexican army fired its cannons at the Alamo. There were now eight Mexican cannons aimed at the mission from the west and south. The Texians did not return fire. Ammunition was running low. They had orders to hold their fire.

## A Bagpipe and Fiddle

Davy Crockett decided to take the defenders' minds off the freezing weather and their situation. He found an old fiddle and challenged bagpiper John McGregor to a duel. It was time to see who could make the most noise. They took turns playing as loud as they could. The rest of the men laughed and cheered. For a while, the Texians even forgot that

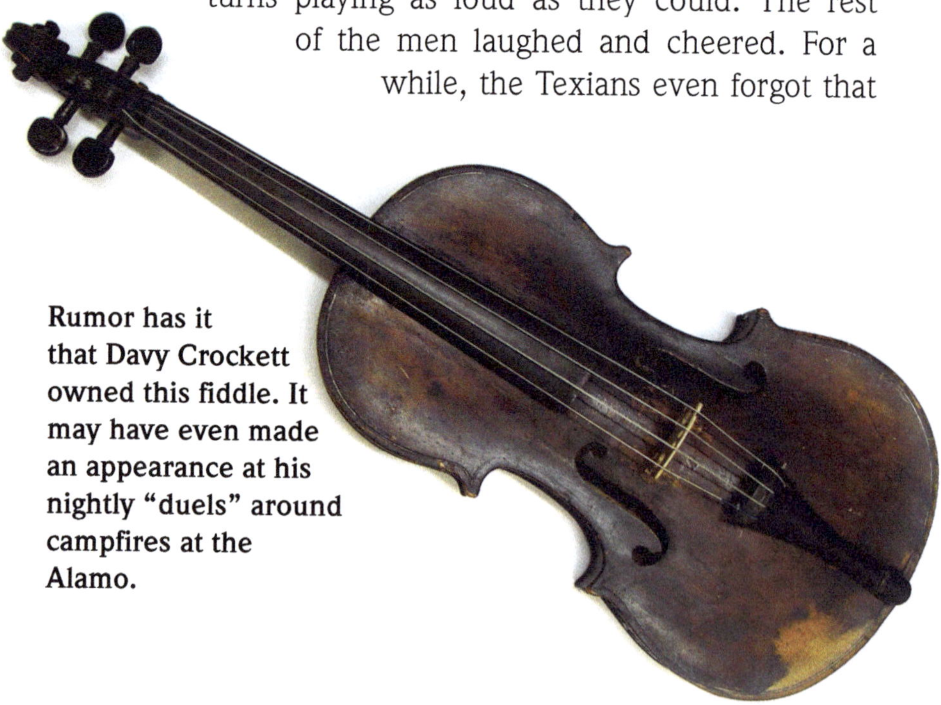

**Rumor has it that Davy Crockett owned this fiddle. It may have even made an appearance at his nightly "duels" around campfires at the Alamo.**

the Mexican army was just on the other side of the mission walls. The contest was popular. Crockett and McGregor repeated the musical duel each night around the campfire.

## Reinforcements for Santa Anna and Help from Gonzales

More Mexican troops marched into San Antonio on February 26. Cannons were now aimed at three sides of the Alamo. The water supply from the irrigation ditch was cut off. The Texians had to depend on a new well they had dug.

Bowie was too sick to get up, but he had men carry his cot out to the troops. He urged everyone to keep fighting no matter what happened. From inside, the men could only watch and wait. They hoped help would arrive in time.

That afternoon, the Texian lookouts yelled and pointed. A Mexican general rode along the line of enemy troops. Aides and officers surrounded him. The Texians fired at him, but no one hit the target. The general was Santa Anna.

On February 29, the Alamo defenders aimed their cannons. They fired at the house Santa Anna used as his headquarters. They hit the target but caused little damage. No Mexican officers were killed or wounded.

Shortly after midnight, John Smith arrived from Gonzales. He brought thirty-two volunteers. These men were farmers and businessmen, not soldiers. George Washington Cottle, for example, had a wife and children waiting in Gonzales. Marcus L. Sewell had just arrived from England. But they had come to help.

They had no problems until they reached the Alamo walls. A nervous Texian fired one shot at the group. It hit one volunteer in the foot. Despite this, they were ready to defend the Alamo, to fight Santa Anna and the army of Mexico.

The reinforcements lifted the spirits of the Texians inside the Alamo, but only briefly. They were cut off from the outside world. They wanted news. They hoped Fannin and Houston were on the way with help. But they had no way of knowing if others were coming to their aid.

Davy Crockett told Susanna Dickinson, "I think we had better march out and die in the open air. I don't like to be hemmed up."[4]

As the days passed, the Texians realized they could not hold out very long without help. The old mission was hard to defend. Though the rebels had done what they could, the outer walls were weak. They would not hold up to constant attack from the Mexican cannons. The walls were also not as tall as the ones on most forts. Mexican troops could easily scale them. They provided little protection for riflemen. There were no holes to fire through. The Texians had to stand up to aim and fire. Their heads and shoulders became targets for Mexican soldiers.

The situation inside the Alamo grew more uncertain every day. Gunpowder was in short supply. Nineteen cannons guarded the walls, but they were far too small to send the Mexican army running.

Reinforcements were needed now. The 189 rebels inside the Alamo knew that was their only hope. To hold out against Santa Anna and his army, more Texians had to take a stand beside the men already inside the Alamo.

## Independence!

Texas was a territory of Mexico when Santa Anna marched into San Antonio. The Mexican flag flew over the Alamo as the siege began.

On March 1, 1836, a convention gathered at Washington-on-the-Brazos. The delegates went to work immediately. By the next day, they had drafted a declaration of independence. Each delegate used an eagle quill to sign his name. They raised the lone-star flag. It stood for the new Republic of Texas.

Three Tejanos—Lorenzo de Zavala, Don Francisco Ruiz, and Don Antonio Navarro—attended the meeting. They signed the declaration along with the other Texians. They were courageous to rebel and stand up against Santa Anna.

Later that day, news reached the convention. Thirty men from Gonzales had gone to the Alamo. They went to fight with the Texians inside the fort. But thirty men were not enough. It would take an army of Texians to defeat Santa Anna.

The next day, a message arrived from Travis. Many delegates wanted to take up arms and hurry to San Antonio. Houston persuaded them not to go. He knew that the delegates' work was not done. They had to create a new government for Texas. They could not afford to rush off and be heroes. It was a hard decision for Houston to make. He had to choose between the future of the new republic and the lives of the small band of Texians defending the Alamo.

## Fannin to the Rescue

On February 27, the second plea for help had reached Goliad. Fannin read the message from Travis. He understood that the Alamo's situation was desperate. He then ordered his troops to prepare to march immediately.

Before he left, Fannin sent a message to Gonzales. He explained that he was on his way to the Alamo with

# Living Together

The people of Texas were not all immigrants from America. Spanish soldiers and missionaries settled in the territory. Many Native Americans claimed lands in Texas. These different groups lived side by side. Over the years, men and women from the different groups married each other. The children of these marriages became known as Tejanos. Some of the volunteers inside the Alamo were Tejanos.

Juan Seguín was a leader of the Tejano rebels. He was inside the Alamo with the Texas rebels when Santa Anna marched into San Antonio. He helped to defend the old mission during the first few days of the siege. Then, Travis sent Seguín for reinforcements. He rallied a band of men in Gonzales, but they did not reach the Alamo in time.

Texas won independence with Seguín's help. But his Texas friends quickly forgot that he fought with them. They ran him out of Texas when the war ended. He was forced to live out his days in Mexico.

This statue sits at the site of Juan Seguín's burial in Seguin, Texas.

330 men. He wanted to meet up with more volunteers. Together they would march on San Antonio.

In Gonzales, men responded to the call. Juan Seguín and twenty-five Tejanos set out. They planned to join Fannin and his troops from Goliad.

Fannin marched out on February 28. He had more than three hundred men. They loaded four field cannons onto wagons pulled by oxen. Their ammunition supply was low, but they took what they had.

## Crossing the Line

Inside the Alamo, Travis called his men together. He explained their choices. They could surrender, attempt to escape, or fight to the finish. One story claims that Travis pulled his sword from its sheath and drew a long line in the dirt. He asked every man who was determined to stay here and die with him to cross the line.[5] All but one stepped across the line. Even Bowie demanded that the men carry his cot across the line.

The one man who did not stay was Louis Moses Rose. He took his small bundle of clothes, climbed over the wall, and fled along the river. Everyone else settled down inside the wall of the old mission. Now, Travis, Bowie, Crockett, and the Texians inside the Alamo could only wait for Santa Anna's next move.

6

# VICTORY OR DEATH

On March 3, the church bells rang. From inside the Alamo, the Texians watched as a thousand more Mexican troops with eight large cannons marched in San Antonio. The small band of rebels believed as many as six thousand Mexicans had gathered outside the walls.[1]

Travis sent one last letter to Governor Henry Smith and Sam Houston: "The enemy have kept up a bombardment ... The spirits of my men are still high though they have had much to depress them ... unless it [aid] arrives soon, I shall have to fight the enemy on his own terms ..."[2]

Travis ended with a note that more enemy troops arrived each day. The blood-red flag still waved over the church tower. Everyone knew this meant certain death, but the threat of "no-quarter" had only strengthened the courage of his men: "I feel confident that the ... courage ... [of] my men will not fail them in the last struggle; and although they may be sacrificed ... the victory will cost the enemy so dear, that it will be worse for him than defeat ... God and Texas—Victory or Death!"[3]

## Prepared to Die

Many of the rebels wrote final letters home. No one expected to survive. They had come to Texas for many reasons. Some were middle-aged and hoping to start over. One young defender from north of the Ohio River explained: "[If] we succeed, the Country is ours, it is immense in extent and fertile in its soil."[4]

Travis sent one personal note. He had a seven-year-old son who was being cared for by friends: "Take care of my little boy ... And [if] I should perish, he will have nothing but the proud recollection that he is the son of a man who died for his country."[5]

Later that day, Susanna and Angelina Dickinson visited Travis. He gave young Angelina a gift. It was a gold ring set with a black stone. He hung it on a string and put it around her neck. He told her to keep it safe.

Davy Crockett put on clothes washed by the women in the fort. He told everyone he wanted to die in clean clothing so he might have a decent burial.[6]

## The Alamo Must Fall

Santa Anna had planned to defeat the Texians quickly. It was a matter of honor. He needed to reclaim the Alamo for Mexico. Also, San Antonio blocked an important route into the heart of Mexico. The general expected that his army would capture the fort within a few days. But he could not attack immediately. This was partly because he needed his large 12-pound (5 kg) cannons.

While he waited, Santa Anna planned every detail of the siege. He positioned soldiers around the Alamo and ordered them to keep up a steady fire. It went on all day long. He ordered others to build earthworks for the cannons that were on the way. He moved troops regularly. Each time his line drew closer to the old mission walls. When two batteries of cannons arrived, he had them placed about 1,000 feet (305 m) from the mission. Each battery had four small guns. The general watched as they opened fire. Santa Anna sent officers to search farms. His army needed grain, cattle, and hogs. He even went scouting with a small cavalry unit. His officers worried that he was doing too much himself.

## Texians to the Rescue

On February 28, some of Santa Anna's scouts returned. They had important information. Colonel Fannin was marching from Goliad with more than two hundred men.

This forced Santa Anna to change his plans. Soldiers had to be sent to stop Fannin from reaching the Alamo. Most of Santa Anna's troops still had not arrived. The general sent cavalry to watch the road from Goliad. He pulled men from the lines around the mission walls. Santa Anna supplied them with ten cases of ammunition. They were ordered to march east. He gave one final order. His officers were to take no prisoners.

The troops prepared to march. They picked up their muskets and left as night fell. With fewer Mexican soldiers to surround the Alamo, the line was thin. The men spread out and tried to close the gaps. By midnight, another winter

Colonel Fannin rallied over two hundred men to help those Texians fighting at the Alamo, but problems soon after starting the jouney had him and his troops abandoning the mission.

storm blew in. The weather made it hard for the soldiers to see or hear anything. That night, it would have been easy for the Texians to slip through the line and escape.

The Mexican troops on the road to Goliad marched east but saw no signs of the Texian reinforcements. When Santa Anna got this message, he called them back to San Antonio. He focused again on the siege.

## Fannin Retreats

Fannin ran into problems almost immediately after he left Goliad. Three wagons broke down in the first two hours. A half mile (0.8 km) from the fort, the Texians had to cross the San Antonio River swollen by heavy rains. The oxen could not drag the wagons across. It took all afternoon to empty the wagons and move the guns across safely. Now, they had another problem. The guns were across the river, but the wagons loaded with ammunition were still on the other side.

It was late in the day, so Fannin decided to make camp. The next morning, they found that the oxen and horses had wandered off. Faced with all these problems, Fannin called his officers together for a council of war. Before the officers made any decisions, five men rode up reporting that the Mexican army was only 50 miles (80 km) away. With a Mexican force nearby, Fannin needed to protect the people of Goliad. He turned back, away from San Antonio and the Alamo.

## Last Call for Help

Travis sent more messages to Fannin. In one message, Travis said he would fire a cannon morning, noon, and night. That would show that the Texians inside the Alamo still

This statue of James Butler Bonham stands in Bonham, Texas, a city named after the legendary figure.

## Fight or Surrender

After James Butler Bonham brought news on March 3 that Fannin would not send troops to the Alamo, the defenders discussed options. A plan to escape and the possibility of surrender were considered.

The volunteers were divided. Should they surrender to Santa Anna before he attacked? Or should they attempt to escape in the night? Both of these choices undermined a strong undivided defense of the Alamo.

Bowie, Crockett, and other volunteers were in favor of a last-minute attempt to negotiate with Santa Anna. Travis was determined to stay and fight to the last man.[7] It would buy more time for the new Texas government.

held out. Colonel James Bonham delivered one message in person. He asked Fannin to try one final time to get to the Alamo with his troops. Fannin refused. Instead, he tried to talk Bonham out of going back to San Antonio. He told the young man it would mean certain death.

Bonham spat on the ground. He told Fannin that Travis deserved a reply. Then, he promised to report the results of his mission or die trying. Bonham left Goliad and reached the Alamo on the morning of March 3. By this time, the Mexican army had closed in around the fort. Bonham was determined to get his news to Travis. The messenger tied a white handkerchief onto his hat. That sign told the men inside the fort that he was a friend. He leaned low over his horse's back and rode through the picket lines, surprising the Mexicans. They grabbed their guns and opened fire, but Bonham made it safely inside the walls of the mission.

Bonham quickly told Travis the bad news. Now, the commander knew the worst. They were completely surrounded by the Mexican army and no more help was on the way.

## A Night Filled with Noise

Santa Anna had another plan. He wanted to harass the Texians inside the Alamo. He filled every night with noise. He ordered his band to blare their horns and trumpets. This "music" was accompanied by cheers, gunshots, and the blast of grenades and cannon. The rebels found it difficult to sleep through the racket.

As the days passed, the Mexicans were worn down, too. There were few supplies in San Antonio. Everything Santa Anna's army needed was on his wagon train. The wagons were following at the rear of the troops. They were still marching north. Santa Anna sent more messengers to hurry them along. The generals in charge found it difficult to hurry the foot soldiers. They were tired. They did not have enough water. They marched along roads lined with dead mules and oxen, smashed cases, and wrecked carts.

Santa Anna also sent a messenger to Mexico City. He reported the successful capture of San Antonio, failing to mention one troublesome fact. He said not a single word about the Texians who still defended the Alamo.

## Time to Strike

By March 4, 1836, Santa Anna decided to wait no longer for the Texians to give up. It was time to teach the rebels a lesson. The victory would bring him glory. Recapturing the Alamo would be a small skirmish, but it was part of the larger battle. Santa Anna planned to return the territory of Texas to Mexican control.

On the evening of March 4, Santa Anna ordered his generals to report to headquarters. He asked them if the time was right to take the Alamo by storm. Two generals were ready to attack. Others, however, wanted to wait. General Cos had lost the Alamo to the Texians. He knew the old mission well. He thought more cannons should be in place before they attacked. Another officer pointed out that they were still short on doctors and medical supplies.

Santa Anna listened briefly to their arguments and then dismissed the officers. He had heard enough. He would make the final decision. He wanted to capture the Alamo before a stronger force could come to the rebels' rescue.

By the next afternoon, Santa Anna's plan was complete. His soldiers were to move into place under the cover of darkness. They would be at the walls of the Alamo before the Texians realized what was happening.

Four columns of troops would attack the Alamo at the same time. The cavalry would be sent to the east. It would be their job to cut down any Texians who tried to escape. Santa Anna himself would control the reserves. He would send them in where needed.

The attack would begin at dawn on the morning of March 6. Everything would be ready by that time. Messengers raced from post to post that afternoon. They delivered copies of Santa Anna's orders. By five o'clock that evening, soldiers were getting ready, moving into position. Three hours later, the men settled down for a long night of waiting. They munched on rations of hardtack and then bedded down. At midnight, officers moved among the soldiers. They woke them up and mustered them into line. At his headquarters, Santa Anna gulped a cup of coffee and reviewed the last details of his attack.

At one in the morning, the four columns moved out. They marched toward the old mission walls. The only sound was the dull tramp of feet on dirt.

An hour before the attack, the cavalry saddled up and rode out of town. The Mexican troops settled down within yards of the Alamo. They were lying on the ground, waiting.

At five o'clock, it was still dark enough so that it was hard to see. The bugler waited for a signal from Santa Anna to sound the attack.

7

# THE BUGLE SOUNDS

Santa Anna's bugler sounded the attack before daylight on the morning of March 6, 1836. Captain John Baugh heard the bugle and tried to spot the Mexicans through the darkness. The noises Baugh heard could mean only one thing: The Mexicans were attacking the Alamo. He sounded the alarm.

The Texians inside the Alamo raced to their posts. Travis was still in bed. He jumped up and grabbed his sword and shotgun. As the commander ran outside, rockets exploded in the sky.

Travis, armed with his sword and double-barreled shotgun, hurried to the north wall. The Mexicans were already closing in on that side of the Alamo. They had reached the ditch just outside the wall. They were too close for the cannons to fire on them.

The Mexican soldiers carried ten ladders. They placed them against the wall and began to climb. Travis leaned over the parapet. He aimed his shotgun down at the enemy. As he pulled the trigger, shots were fired from the darkness

## Bugles in Battle

During Texas's war for independence, armies used bugle calls to send orders to troops spread out across the battlefield. Bugles could be heard for long distances. Different calls told soldiers to attack or to retreat. When the order to attack was sounded, all soldiers could hear the call and charged forward together.

On the morning of March 6, 1836, Santa Anna ordered his army band to play the *degüello*. The music was the signal to attack the Alamo. The word "degüello" means the act of beheading or throat-cutting. In Spanish history, this battle music meant complete destruction of the enemy without mercy.[1]

below. One bullet found its mark. It hit Travis in the forehead. He fell backward and rolled down the earthen bank. Travis died instantly, with his shotgun still clutched in his hand.[2]

All along the walls of the Alamo, the rebels fired at the Mexican soldiers. As heads appeared at the top, Texian riflemen picked them off. Every Texian had four or five rifles at his side so he could shoot quickly without reloading. Captain Dickinson was in charge of the cannons. His men sent blast after blast into the troops moving toward them. On the east and south, the cannon fire stopped the Mexicans. Blasts knocked soldiers over like they were straws.

Santa Anna watched from a distance. Flashes from guns, cannons, and rockets lit up the old mission. Three of the

The scene of Santa Anna's attack on the Texian troops at the Alamo is depicted in this drawing.

four Mexican columns had ended up near the north wall. These men pushed forward and then fell back. The troops at the north wall were protected from the Alamo cannons. But they were not safe from the rifles and muskets of their own countrymen. One officer reported the effects of the friendly fire: "Since they [the Mexican army] attacked in a close column, the shots were aimed at the backs of those ahead of them ... The soldiers under the wall were raked time and again by the bullets of their friends."[3]

The confusion alarmed Santa Anna.[4] He sent in his reserves. He also ordered his officers to go with them. The next wave of Mexicans charged. They fired blindly as they ran. By this time, about fifteen hundred Mexican soldiers pressed toward the north wall. There were as many as five hundred dead soldiers under their feet. They climbed over the bodies as they tried again to scale the walls.

Davy Crockett and his twelve sharpshooters who'd come with him from Tennessee manned a post on the opposite side of the fort. They held off the first attack, but the tide soon turned against them. Enrique Esparza was a boy inside the Alamo during the attack. He survived the battle and later recounted Crockett's brave fight: "He [Crockett] was everywhere ...and personally slew many of the enemy with his rifle, pistol, and his knife. He fought hand to hand. He clubbed his rifle when they closed in on him and knocked them down with its stock ... He fought to his last breath ... When he died there was a heap of slain [Mexican soldiers] in front and on each side of him. Those he had all killed before he finally fell on top of the heap."[5]

A Mexican soldier described Crockett's death. He said that a soldier struck Crockett above the right eye with a

**The Battle of the Alamo, as it's called today, involved every Texian man that could fight. This scene illustrates the final hours of the conflict in March 1836 from the Texian's perspective. Some men were dressed in top hats, while others wore animal skins. They all fought until their last breath.**

sword. The Texian from Tennessee fell to the ground and was instantly stabbed by twenty bayonets.

## Over the Walls

With most of the Mexican troops at the north wall, many Texians went to lend a hand. This left other sections exposed. The Mexicans soon attacked a low part in the south wall. In minutes, they seized the 18-pound cannon. They killed the gun crew then raced down the ramp inside the Alamo.

More Mexican troops streamed over the wall into the plaza. Their numbers were too much for the Texians inside the Alamo, who fled over the wall in an attempt to escape. The Mexican cavalry was waiting for them. They swept down on horseback, hacking at the men with swords. The Texians fought back. Two managed to escape temporarily. One hid under a bush. He was discovered and stabbed to death. Another hid under a bridge. A Tejano woman who was not part of the rebel cause reported his whereabouts. He, too, was killed.

## Fight to the End

There was a glow in the east, but the sun was still not up. More soldiers scrambled over the north wall. Texas riflemen fired down at them from the roof of the barracks. Soon, there were so many Mexican soldiers in the plaza below that it was hard to miss. The Mexicans ran around stabbing defenders with bayonets. The Texians fought back with knives. They used their rifles like clubs.

Finally, the Texians retreated. They holed up in rooms and prepared for a last-ditch defense. The doorways were blocked with walls made of earth. The walls were just high enough to rest a rifle. The Texians fired over the mounds of dirt and through holes in the walls and doorways. Mexicans in the plaza ducked for cover. But the plaza offered little protection and many died.

At the south end of the plaza, the Mexicans turned the 18-pound cannon and aimed it at the Texians behind the barricades. One blast knocked in the walls. Mexican soldiers burst into the rooms. They fired at random, hitting both friend and foe.

The Battle of the Alamo was a bloody exchange between Texian and Mexican forces. Many paintings depict the action and carnage, like this one.

One wounded Texian grabbed a torch. He headed for the gunpowder room inside the chapel. He planned to blow up the Alamo. However, he was killed by a bullet before he reached his goal. Many Texians died in the barracks facing the plaza. It took an hour for the Mexicans to clear out the rooms.

Now, only Captain Dickinson and his cannon crew were left to defend the Alamo. They manned the 12-pound cannon on a high platform behind the chapel. He rushed into the chapel, looking for his wife. "Good God, Sue, the Mexicans are inside our walls!" he shouted. "If they spare you, save my child."[6] He kissed her then raced back to his crew of ten. Dickinson was killed shortly afterward. James Bonham and the others manning the cannon were also killed. One gunner took his own life. He picked up a child from the chapel floor below. With the child in his arms, he jumped from the platform. Both were killed by the fall.[7]

Three other gunners tried to retreat to the chapel. Mexican soldiers killed them all. One died an extremely painful death. He was picked up by the soldiers' bayonets like a pig on a skewer. They tossed him up and down until he died.

The Mexicans found Jim Bowie lying in bed. Legend has it that he began shooting as the Mexicans crashed into his room. But he was very sick and probably could not have fired a gun.

Madam Candelaria, the woman who was nursing Bowie, gave this account. She reported that Colonel Bowie was already dead when the Mexicans entered the Alamo. "One of them thrust a bayonet into the lifeless head of Colonel Bowie and lifted his body from my lap."[8]

Bowie's sister-in-law, Juana Alsbury, was also at the Alamo. She did not learn of his death until the battle was over. She and her sister were in a small room near the chapel. Alsbury sent her sister to ask the Mexican soldiers not to fire into their room.

The soldiers greeted her request with curses and tore the shawl from her shoulders. Alsbury was standing nearby with her baby. She wondered if she was about to die.[9] The soldiers took money and valuables from their trunk. They did not harm the women but sent them into the Alamo plaza. A Mexican officer found them soon after that. He took them to a place where they would be safe.

## Women and Children

General Cos tried to end the killing. He ordered his bugler to blow the cease-fire signal. The soldiers paid no attention. In the Alamo chapel, Susanna Dickinson crouched against the wall with her daughter wrapped in her apron. She had a minor leg wound from a musket ball. Soldiers burst in, clearly out of control. Three young boys were killed as Susanna Dickinson watched. She feared that she and her daughter would be next. Instead, the soldiers ordered her to move to a corner. Before long, other women and children joined her.

Enrique Esparza was sitting beside his father's body. Years later, Esparza reported what happened next: "For fully a quarter of an hour they [the Mexican soldiers] kept firing after all the defenders had been slain and their corpses were lying still."[10]

## They Died for Texas Independence!

The battle that began just before sunrise ended by 6:30 that same morning. Santa Anna sent more than fifteen hundred soldiers into battle. About six hundred Mexican soldiers died or were wounded.[11] Every last Texian soldier was dead. General Santa Anna had said "no quarter—no mercy—no surrender." None was given. The battle for the Alamo was over.

When the men of the Alamo made their last stand, they did not know Texas had declared independence on March 2, 1836. However, they were in favor of independence. In fact, they had sent men to represent them at the convention, telling them to vote for an independent Texas.

## No Quarter

By 6:30 on the morning of March 6, the Mexicans had stopped shooting and bayoneting bodies. The much larger Mexican force had overrun 189 rebels. The Alamo was quiet. Fires burned here and there. Now, a flag of red, white, and green billowed in the morning breeze. The fierce eagle of Mexico soared proudly at its center.

8

# SAN ANTONIO RECLAIMED

Barely an hour had passed since the bugle call. As the smoke cleared, the early morning light illuminated the battlefield. It was a grisly scene. Dead bodies, severed limbs, and blood was everywhere. Santa Anna entered the Alamo to survey the carnage. The army band played a lively march to announce his arrival. One Mexican officer approached the general, leading five Texian prisoners.[1] The general reprimanded him for not killing them on the spot. He turned his back and walked away. The soldiers drew their swords. They tortured and killed the rebels.[2]

Many of the Mexican officers were amazed by how well the handful of Texians had defended the Alamo.[3] They had fought a good battle. The victory had taken a toll on the Mexican army. Santa Anna had lost many men. But he said of the battle, "It was but a small affair."[4]

Santa Anna asked to see the bodies of Jim Bowie, William Travis, and David Crockett. Travis's slave, Joe, pointed out his dead master. Colonel Bowie was found in his bed in a room on the south side. Crockett's body was near the Alamo chapel where the defenders had made a last stand.

## How Did Crockett Die?

The question of how Davy Crockett died has been hotly debated. He came to Texas to make a new start, not to fight. Crockett quickly discovered that he liked the country. On January 9, he wrote in a letter home that Texas is "the garden spot of the world ... and I do believe it is a fortune for any man to come here."[5]

Crockett saw the political advantages of taking up arms in defense of the new Texas government. He volunteered to defend the Alamo.

Accounts of Crockett's death have grown into legends and likely been exaggerated. Mexican Sergeant Felix Nuñez believed he saw a man who fit Crockett's description fall. "Of the many soldiers who took deliberate aim at him and fired, not one ever hit him. On the contrary, he never missed a shot."[6]

Bowie's nurse claimed Crockett stopped an entire regiment from coming over the barricade. "[A] storm of bullets rained against the walls. Every man fell at the door but Crockett. I could see him struggling with the head of the column ... I saw Crocket fall backwards."

After the battle, Susanna Dickinson saw Crockett near the chapel door "lying dead and mutilated ... I remember seeing his peculiar cap by his side."[7]

**This illustration shows Texian and Mexican troops coming together in combat during the Battle of the Alamo. Women and children are among those caught in the action.**

Santa Anna wrote a brief report. He sent it to Mexico City. "Victory belongs to the army which, at this moment, 8 o'clock A.M., achieved a complete and glorious triumph that will render its memory imperishable."[8]

## Free to Go

The women and children were marched from the chapel through the piles of dead Mexicans and Texians. They were taken to the house of a Tejano family loyal to the Mexican government. The family fed and cared for them.

Later in the day, Santa Anna interviewed the women. He talked with each of them individually. Santa Anna met with Susanna Dickinson. He offered to adopt her daughter, Angelina. She refused to give up her child. Santa Anna then gave her two pesos and a blanket. He also told her that she was free to go.

## Burn the Dead

Santa Anna gave Francisco Ruiz, the mayor of San Antonio, a nasty job. He was to remove the dead bodies. Loyal Mexican soldiers would be buried in the local cemetery. The rebels were to be burned.

The villagers brought carts to haul the soldiers to the cemetery. The graveyard was small. There was not enough space for all the dead soldiers. Ruiz reported that he had some of them thrown in the river.[9]

Next, the villagers were sent to collect wood from the countryside. By the middle of the afternoon, they started piling up the dry branches. Bodies of the dead Texian rebels were placed on top of the wood. Then, more branches were added to the pile. This was followed by another layer of bodies. The piles were set afire before the sun set.

The mayor witnessed all of this. He reported that the bodies were burned in three piles. A local teenager watched the bodies burning: "I saw an immense pillar of fire shoot up south and east of the Alamo, and dense smoke from it rose high into the clouds."[10] The stink from the burning flesh filled the air for two days.

The next day, a villager came to look at what was left after the fires had died out. He saw bits of bones and

Susanna Dickinson was one of the survivors of the Battle of the Alamo. She lived on to tell what she saw and experienced that fateful day.

## The Ones Who Walked Away

Louis Moses Rose had walked away from the Alamo three days before the final battle. Later, he was often asked why he did not stay in the Alamo with the others. Rose always replied, "I wasn't ready to die."[11]

After meeting with Santa Anna, Susanna Dickinson, other women and children, and Jim Bowie's slave, Joe, left quickly. They walked away from San Antonio, taking little with them besides the sad story of the Alamo's fall. Santa Anna wanted news of the Alamo to spread throughout Texas. He wanted all Texians to know what would happen to them if they continued to rebel.

charred flesh. These were the last remains of all the Texians who had made a stand at the Alamo.

## After the Fall of the Alamo

Texians in other parts of the territory were waiting for news from the Alamo. Those who lived nearby listened for the sound of cannon fire. Travis had promised to fire his big gun three times each day as long he held the Alamo. Those listening were disappointed. No shots were heard. From a distance, though, they did see the plume of smoke. It drifted into the air near San Antonio.

By March 10, in Washington-on-the-Brazos, members of the convention were worried. One member said: "It is much feared that Travis and company are all massacred."[12]

The next day, General Houston set out for San Antonio. He took one hundred volunteers with him. Houston first got news of the Alamo when he reached Gonzales. Two Tejanos had arrived in town. They reported that all the defenders had been killed. Houston sent a trusted scout, Deaf Smith, to confirm the facts. Along the way, the scouting party met Susanna, Joe, and the other survivors from the Alamo. Now, there was no doubt.

Word reached the convention on March 15. The news shocked people everywhere. General Houston took the news especially hard. He felt responsible.[13] He had failed to send help to the Alamo in time to save the brave defenders.

At first, many could not believe what had happened at the Alamo. The women of Gonzales were the first to accept the truth. They had sent their husbands to the Alamo. Thirty-two men had gone to help. They were not coming back. Everyone in Gonzales felt the loss. Even as they mourned, they began to pack up. They feared that Santa Anna was headed for Gonzales. They hurried east to escape the Mexican army.

All across the territory, settlers began to leave. They did not want to be caught in the path of Santa Anna's army. David Ayers left his home in Montville. He had little Charlie Travis with him. He had promised William Travis, Charlie's father, to keep him safe. Now, he had another task to do. Ayers had to break the news to the boy that his father was not coming back.[14]

That night Sam Houston wrote to Fannin in Goliad. In the letter, he said: "I have little doubt that the Alamo has fallen . . . Colonel Travis intended firing signal guns at three different periods of each day until [help] should arrive. No signal guns have been heard since Sunday, though a scouting party [has] just returned who approached within twelve miles [19 km] of it, and remained there forty-eight hours."[15]

Houston ordered Fannin to fall back. He was to move his command to Victoria. They were to take all the artillery they could carry. The remainder was to be sunk in the river. Houston also ordered Fannin to see that no women and children were left behind in Goliad.

The general ended with the following instructions: "You will take the necessary measures to blow up that fortress . . . The immediate advance of the enemy may be confidently expected . . . Prompt movements are therefore highly important."[16]

9

# THE REPUBLIC OF TEXAS

After March 2, Texians prepared for battle. The declaration of independence was also a declaration of war with Mexico. Now, Texas had to act like an independent country. The rebels' actions so far had drawn the wrath of General Santa Anna and the full force of his well-trained Mexican army. As Texas prepared to fight back, the new government faced many problems. There was no treasury. Most of its population was on the run from the Mexican army. Half of the Texas army had already been captured and killed. But there was no backing down. No one could forget the brave men who had already died for Texas independence. The Texians marched into battle, waving a new flag and rallying to the battle cry: "Remember the Alamo!"

Fannin delayed his retreat a few days. He rescued settlers in the town of Refugio. They were in the path of Mexican troops. The Texas troops finally set out from Goliad on March 19. Mexican cavalrymen were not far behind. They caught up with the Texians on the open prairie. Fannin's force was outnumbered four to one. They fought all afternoon and into the night. By the next morning, Fannin had to surrender.

The Texians were taken back to Goliad and held captive for a week. Then, on March 27, all 390 were marched away from town. They expected to be sent back to the United States. Instead, 342 men were killed. When some men tried to run, soldiers cut them down with swords. Still, some managed to escape. Others were spared because they were doctors, mechanics, or interpreters.

Word of Fannin's fate swept across the country. Two other small rebel forces were also captured and killed. Santa Anna was doing what he said he would: He had promised to kill or to drive out every American from Texas.

## Texians on the Run

As the Mexican army advanced, Texians fled from their homes. They raced back toward the border of the United States. They left beds unmade and breakfast on the table. Some took whatever could be carried on wagons or oxcarts. Many were on foot. Women carried babies in their arms.

Driven by fear, settlers walked through the wet weather and the Texas mud to escape the Mexican army.[1] Many got sick and died. This race to safety was later called the "Great Runaway Scrape."[2]

## Retreat

A large Mexican force was marching toward Gonzales. General Sam Houston decided to retreat. He had the town burned along with any supplies he could not take with him. There were not enough wagons to haul all his cannons. Those left behind were sunk in the river so the enemy could not use them.

Houston's retreat did not make anyone happy. Texas officials wanted him to fight. His troops and officers

## Flags for the Texas Republic

The first flag of the Republic of Texas may have been designed by Lorenzo de Zavala. It featured a large white star in the center of a blue field. Letters at each point of the star spelled out TEXAS. The "Zavala flag" was allegedly adopted in the Convention of 1836 at Washington-on-the-Brazos. Unfortunately, written journals of the convention show no record that the convention accepted Zavala's design. Still, some historians consider the "Zavala flag" the first Texas flag.

The first official flag was adopted by the Congress of the Republic and approved by President Sam Houston on December 10, 1836. The "National Standard of Texas" was an azure background with a large golden star in the center. This flag, designed by David G. Burnet, served as the national flag until January 25, 1839.[3]

**The first flag of Texas was designed in 1836.**

complained, too. They were tired of running. Some were so unhappy they deserted, or left, the army.[4] Still, Houston refused to stand and fight. He continued his march across the Texas prairies.

On April 18, 1836, Houston and his troops reached Harrisburg, Texas. The Mexican army was already in the area. Scout Deaf Smith captured two Mexican messengers. They carried news of Santa Anna. Houston learned that the general had camped in a town located between the Texians and the Gulf of Mexico.

The next morning, Houston marched south. He left behind extra supplies for the men who were sick. He set out for Lynch's Ferry on the San Jacinto River. Houston pushed his men hard into the night. He did not call for a halt or allow his men to rest until after midnight. Some dropped out of the march, too tired to go on. After resting them for only two hours, Houston ordered his men to set out again. By daylight, they had reached Lynch's Ferry.

Houston took up a position on the banks of a bayou. Many trees grew along the water's edge. They provided cover for his men. The bayou and the San Jacinto River made a natural barrier to the left and right sides of the Texas troops. The location also offered a good view of the prairie that stretched out for miles.

## Battle of San Jacinto

In the afternoon, the Mexican army marched onto the prairie. Santa Anna lined up his army. He had them face the row of trees. He knew his enemy had taken cover there. He wanted to attack the Texians immediately. It was time to finish this job. He moved a cannon forward. He sent out cavalry riders to protect the gunners. While they shelled the woods, the Mexican infantry advanced. They were ready to attack.

Houston now had two cannons in place. He returned fire. All afternoon, the Mexicans and Texians exchanged cannon fire. Then, some Texians made a direct attack. They tried to take the Mexican cannon but failed to capture it. The attack did force the Mexicans to pull back to the safety of their own line. The day ended with little bloodshed.

About nine o'clock the next morning, General Cos arrived. He had four to five hundred men with him. Now, there were about thirteen hundred Mexican soldiers. Houston had some eight hundred volunteers with him. The Texians waited, but the Mexicans did not attack.

Finally, Houston called a council of war. They voted to attack the next morning. Houston listened to his officers and then made his own decision.[5]

## A Red Flag for the Alamo

At three o'clock in the afternoon on April 21, 1836, Houston ordered the army to "arm and line," meaning to arm themselves with weapons and line up for battle.[6] Houston sent men to destroy the bridge over the bayou. The Texians' cavalry moved quietly off to the left. Two cannons were pushed within 200 yards (183 m) of the Mexican line. The infantry moved up to easy shooting range. One company had tied a big red handkerchief to a stick. It was a reminder of Santa Anna's red flag at the Alamo.

The sun was low as the Texians moved forward. There was no sign of life from the Mexican camp. An order was given to strike up the band. The band was one fife and an old drum. The cavalry moved in at a trot, then charged. The two cannons blasted away. The infantry fired

This shows the short-lived Battle of San Jacinto in April 1836.

repeatedly and swept into the Mexican camp. As the Texians attacked, some began to yell: "Remember the Alamo!"[7] Others quickly took up the cry.

The afternoon attack was a surprise. Many Mexicans were gathering wood. Others were sleeping in the shade. The Mexican cavalrymen had dismounted. Muskets were stacked. Most officers were in their tents. The Mexicans broke and ran across the prairie. The Texian cavalry raced after them.

The battle was over in eighteen minutes. About six hundred Mexicans were killed or wounded. More than seven hundred prisoners were taken. About forty escaped. Only nine Texians died fighting. Twenty-three others were wounded.

## Defeat

When the Texians struck, Santa Anna was asleep. After the first alarm, he realized that the situation was hopeless. He turned his horse loose and took cover in some trees. He changed his clothes to disguise himself as a foot soldier. After dark, he crossed the bayou and hid in an abandoned cabin. The next day, he tried to slip away. He was spotted, captured, and taken to Houston. The Texian general was resting under a tree. His ankle had been shattered by gunfire during the fighting. When presented to Houston, Santa Anna is said to have made this comment: "Sir, yours is no common destiny; you have captured the Napoleon of the west."[8]

Many Texas soldiers wanted to kill the Mexican general. Houston would not let them. He knew that Santa Anna was more valuable alive than dead. Houston ordered Santa Anna to withdraw from the Texas Territory. He was to take all his troops with him.

Houston also set out terms for a treaty to end the war. Texas would be an independent country. The Rio Grande was to be its southern border. All property taken by the

**This painting imagines the surrender of Santa Anna to Sam Houston and his men after the Battle of San Jacinto.**

Mexican army was to be returned. Prisoners would be exchanged.

Santa Anna agreed to the terms and was released. From there, he returned to Mexico City, but he soon discovered he was no longer president. He had been overthrown. The

## Santa Anna After the War

The disgrace of losing the Texas Revolution did not stop Santa Anna. He went on to reclaim power over Mexico and served as president seven more times between 1839 and 1855.

In 1838, only two years after the Battle of the Alamo, Santa Anna led his army into battle again. The general was wounded and doctors had to amputate his leg. The general kept his leg after surgery. It was first buried at his hacienda, or ranch. However, he dug up the shriveled leg when he became president in 1842. He paraded it to Mexico City on a coach and gave his leg a state funeral. Cannons were fired. Poetry and speeches were read.

In 1847, at the Battle of Cerro Gordo in the Mexican–American War, the Illinois Infantry surprised Santa Anna. The general fled without his artificial cork-and-wood leg. The Illinois soldiers seized the leg and took it home to Illinois. The Mexican government's requests to have the fake limb returned were denied.[9]

Santa Anna died in Mexico City, on June 21, 1876. He was eighty-two years old.

new government rejected the terms of the treaty. This had little effect on Texas, however. The territory had won its independence. Nations around the world accepted it as a country. It was called the Republic of Texas. Houston was elected as the first president. For the next ten years, the citizens of Texas ruled themselves independently.

10

# THE TWENTY-EIGHTH STATE TODAY

Ten years later, the Republic of Texas was annexed by the United States. It became the twenty-eighth state in the union. Mexico had never recognized Texas as an independent country. They claimed the territory still belonged to them. Thus, America and Mexico went to war.

War began on April 25, 1846. Mexican soldiers attacked American troops. The first strike was along the southern border of Texas. General Santa Anna was a commander during this war, too. The United States captured Mexico City on September 14, 1847. That ended the fighting.

The Treaty of Guadalupe–Hidalgo was signed a few months later. This ended the war. Mexico accepted the Rio Grande as the boundary between Texas and Mexico. Mexico also gave the United States more territory. The new territory eventually became the states of California, Nevada, Utah, part of Arizona, and New Mexico.

## The Alamo Remembered

Today, Texas is an important part of the United States. The people who live there have not forgotten their history

## Can Texas Secede?

Texas declared independence from Mexico in 1836. The young country's leaders were interested in becoming a US state then. However, the Republic of Texas did not join the United States until 1845 when Congress approved the Joint Resolution for Annexing Texas to the United States.

This resolution did make it possible for Texas to divide itself into five states of convenient size. This statement has often caused confusion about the state's ability to secede. But the language is clear: Texas can split itself into five new states. It cannot split apart from the United States.

lessons. They are proud of their birthright. They remember that their home was once an independent country. They remember the fight to win their freedom. And they will always "Remember the Alamo."

### What Really Happened at the Alamo?

After the fall of the Alamo, the world wanted to know what had happened. What went on day-to-day inside the walls of the old mission? Much of what occurred during the siege is still cloaked in mystery.

None of the defenders survived the final charge of the Mexicans. The only ones alive to retell the events inside the Alamo were the women, children, slaves, and those few soldiers who left before the final Mexican assault. For

# Texas State Symbols

*Flag:* The Lone Star Flag adopted in 1845

*Nickname:* Lone Star State

*Song:* “Texas, Our Texas”

*Bird:* mockingbird

*Mammal:* Texas longhorn

*Insect:* monarch butterfly

*Flower:* bluebonnet

*Plant:* prickly pear cactus

*Reptile:* Texas horned lizard

most of the battle, the women, children, and slaves were tucked away in the chapel. They did not witness the defeat. This has made it difficult, if not impossible, to determine the facts.

Even today, historians search for answers. They want to know how many defenders were inside the fort. Most now agree that there were 189 men. But that is only a good guess. No list of defenders survived the siege. What is certain is that the Texas rebels were completely outnumbered by the Mexican army. It was an amazing feat for such a small force to hold out for thirteen days.

Did Travis use his sword to draw a line and ask the men to step over it? Susanna Dickinson overheard Travis's last speech to his men. She did not mention a line in the sand. Madam Candelaria also claimed to have witnessed this event. In the version she told, Travis "drew a line on the floor with the point of his sword and asked all who were willing to die for Texas to come over on his side." Only two did not cross the line. One was Bowie. He was too weak to walk. (Some say his cot was carried over the line.) The other was Louis Moses Rose. He "sprang over the wall and disappeared."[1]

Historians generally believe the line in the sand is one of the Alamo's myths. But there is no way to prove without a doubt that it did or did not take place.

One Alamo mystery created more debate than any other. That mystery is where and how Davy Crockett died. Historians are still trying to sort fact from fiction. Susanna Dickinson said she saw Crockett's body lying in the mission plaza. Joe, Travis's slave, showed the body to Santa Anna. Joe said that "Crockett and his friends died together; they were found 'with twenty-four of the enemy dead around them.'"[2] General Cos claimed that Crockett surrendered and tried to avoid death. By his account, Crockett said that he was a foreigner visiting when the battle began.[3] What really occurred is impossible to prove. Answers died with the defenders.

The few facts that survived allow writers and moviemakers to create their own version of tales of the Alamo. They use the facts that can be confirmed. Then, they use their imaginations to fill in the gaps and retell the sad and heroic story of those who died fighting to the last man.

## Destroy It!

When the siege in 1836 ended, Santa Anna ordered his army to get ready to march. Before they moved out, he gave his troops one last task: to destroy the Alamo.

A doctor sent to tend the wounded watched what happened: "They are now as busy as bees ... tearing down the walls," he reported.[4] What could not be pulled down was set on fire. Soon, all that was left were the stone walls of the church.

For many years, no one took care of the Alamo. It was used by different groups. But no effort was made to restore the building. In 1841, Texas gave the mission back to the Catholic Church.

The stars of the 1960 movie *The Alamo* pose for this picture. *The Alamo* is just one of the films made about the battle.

Even then, the mission was often controlled by others. When Texas became the twenty-eighth state, the US government took charge of it. The army used the ruined building for several years. During the Civil War, the Confederacy claimed it. After the Civil War ended, the US government took charge of the Alamo again. It used the old mission until 1876.

On April 23, 1883, the state of Texas purchased the mission from the Catholic Church. The state gave it to the city of San Antonio. Part of the deal was that the city would care for the building.

For the next fifteen years, two women took charge of the Alamo. Clara Driscoll and Adina de Zavala worked together on the project. However, when the two women disagreed, work ended. Driscoll wanted to have the ruin torn down. De Zavala thought the mission should be restored.

Finally, on January 25, 1905, the Texas legislature passed a decree. They asked the Daughters of the Republic of Texas to take care of the historic building. This group still maintains the building and welcomes visitors.

The Alamo has been restored several times. The most important restoration was completed in 1936. It was done for a special celebration. That year, Texas was one hundred years old. The old mission was dedicated as a National Historic Landmark on December 19, 1960.

## The Alamo Today

Today, the Alamo—in downtown San Antonio, Texas—has three buildings to tour: the Shrine, the Long Barrack Museum, and the Gift Museum. There are exhibits about

**Every year, visitors tour the Alamo. It welcomes all people and offers insight into the building and Texas's history.**

the Texas Revolution and Texas history in each building. These displays cover nearly three hundred years of history.

In January 2019, the Long Barrack Exhibit was closed for renovation. "The Church and Long Barrack go back to the early Spanish settlement and mission era, and are the oldest buildings in Texas," Alamo CEO Douglass McDonald said. "We are beginning an evaluation of what is required to . . . protect these buildings for the next millennia."[5]

More than 2.5 million people visit the Alamo each year. They are surprised by how small the old building appears. San Antonio has progressed around the Alamo. Modern skyscrapers surround the mission. The city almost overshadows the site.

Visitors are welcome to walk in the park that surrounds the Alamo. They can still see weapons used during the siege. The famous 18-pound cannon is on display. It was the cannon Travis fired in reply to Santa Anna's blood-red flag.

During a stroll around the grounds, visitors can watch for the "point-of-focus" signs. These displays were designed by illustrator Gary Zaboly. Each sign helps viewers see what the Alamo would have looked like from that spot in March 1836. These signs take visitors back in time. They allow them to relive the siege of the Alamo with the men who bravely defended it.

# CONCLUSION

When the Battle of the Alamo was over, Santa Anna claimed it was but a small affair. The Mexican army had sent more than fifteen hundred soldiers into battle. About six hundred died or were wounded. It seemed that every last Texian soldier was dead. General Santa Anna had promised no quarter, no mercy, no surrender. None was given. For Santa Anna, the battle was over. But the Alamo lived on in the hearts of Texians.

This legendary battle in American history was little more than a massacre. These were scared young men, most far from home. When they tried to surrender, they were cut down by sabers and lances of Mexican cavalrymen outside the Alamo. Mirabau B. Lamar, who commanded the Texas cavalry at San Jacinto, wrote this in a letter to his brother on April 10, 1836: "San Antonio has been retaken and every man in the fort murdered."[1]

Santa Anna sent his battle report to newspapers in the United States. The report stated that many Alamo garrison members had attempted to flee. They were killed by the

**The faces of the soliders involved in the Battle of the Alamo are forever memorialized in this monument, built in 1939. Called out by name are William Travis and Davy Crockett, heroes of the Battle of the Alamo and legends forever connected to the Texas fight for independence from Mexico.**

Mexican cavalry outside the mission's walls. Immediately, the report triggered disbelief and outrage.

One example was published in the May 12, 1836, issue of the *Maryland Gazette*. The editor wrote:

The Gazette of the 23rd March contains the official report of Santa Anna of the capture of the Alamo [and] He reports that after storming the Alamo . . . General Sesma followed the fugitives, who attempted to escape, few if any of whom, remain to tell the tale of their disaster! Was there ever exhibited on the part of a commander of an army such wanton and disgraceful misrepresentation! It is a matter of history that the whole garrison of the Alamo . . . was inhumanly put to the sword within its walls, instead of being pursued by Sesma.[2]

Only two months after the battle, the tale of a heroic last stand had already grown larger than the facts. The defeat at the Alamo also fueled Houston's army. They were determined to overcome the Mexican army. After retreating across Texas ahead of Santa Anna, Texians rallied to the cry, "Remember the Alamo," at the Battle of San Jacinto.

The true story was buried along with the defenders. Once it was clear they had little hope of holding out against Santa Anna's larger force, many defenders tried to escape. With no survivors and few witnesses, the facts were ignored for the most part. The myth of the Alamo captured the public's imagination. The men of the Alamo garrison were recognized as heroes. The Battle of the Alamo was glorified. The epic last stand was created. The story grew into a legend. It symbolized the birth of the new republic and is considered "The Cradle of Texas Liberty."[3]

# CHRONOLOGY

**1824** Mexico passes a new constitution.

**1833** Santa Anna becomes president of Mexico in January.

**1835**

**October 1:** The Battle of Gonzales takes place.

**October 9:** The Texians capture Goliad.

**November:** The Provisional Texas Government is formed.

**December 10:** Texians capture San Antonio and the Alamo.

**1836**

**February 23:** Santa Anna marches into San Antonio, and Texas rebels take shelter in the Alamo.

**February 24–March 5:** The Mexican army besieges the Alamo.

**March 2:** Texas declares its independence.

**March 6:** The Battle of the Alamo takes place.

**Early March:** The Great Runaway Scrape takes place.

**March 17:** The Republic of Texas adopts a constitution.

**March 27:** The Goliad Massacre takes place.

**April 21:** The Battle of San Jacinto takes place.

**1846** Texas is annexed by the United States of America on **April 25**; the Mexican–American War begins when Mexican forces attack American troops stationed along the Texas border.

**1847** United States troops occupy Mexico City on **September 14**.

1848 The Treaty of Guadalupe-Hidalgo is signed on **February 2**, officially ending the Mexican–American War.

1876 Santa Anna dies on **June 21**.

1960 The Alamo is dedicated as a National Historic Landmark on **December 19**.

2019 The Alamo National Historic Landmark Long Barracks close for renovations.

# CHAPTER NOTES


## Introduction

1. James Donovan, *The Blood of Heroes: The 13-Day Struggle for the Alamo—And the Sacrifice That Forged a Nation* (New York, NY: Little, Brown and Company, 2012), p. 255.
2. Texas State Library and Archives Commission, Declaration of Independence of Texas, 1836, https://www.tsl.texas.gov/treasures/republic/declaration.html (accessed April 22, 2019).
3. Donovan, p. 256.

**CHAPTER 1**

## Santa Anna

1. Stephen L. Moore, *Texas Rising: The Epic True Story of the Lone Star Republic and the Rise of the Texas Rangers, 1836–1846* (New York, NY: William Morrow, 2015), p. 100.
2. Ben H. Proctor, *The Battle of the Alamo* (Austin, TX: Texas State Historical Association, 1986), p. 23.
3. Bill Groneman, "Ward, William B.," The Handbook of Texas Online, updated July 23, 2015, https://tshaonline.org/handbook/online/articles/fwabe.
4. Michael A. Lofaro, "Crocket, David," The Handbook of Texas Online, updated October 4, 2017, https://tshaonline.org/handbook/online/articles/fcr24.
5. Thomas Ricks Lindley, *Alamo Traces: New Evidence and New Conclusions* (Lanham, MD: Republic of Texas Press, 2003), pp. 90–91.

**CHAPTER 2**

## Spain Claims Mexico

1. Randolph B. Campbell, *Gone to Texas: A History of the Lone Star State* (New York, NY: Oxford University Press, 2003), p. 42.
2. Richard Bruce Winders, *Sacrificed at the Alamo: Tragedy and Triumph in the Texas Revolution* (Abilene, TX: State House Press, 2004), p. 21.

3. William R. Hunt and John Leffler, “Mills County,” The Handbook of Texas Online, updated January 25, 2019, https://tshaonline.org/handbook/online/articles/hcm14.
4. “Alamo History Chronology,” The Daughters of the Republic of Texas, http://www.drtinfo.org/drt-library/research/alamo-history-chronology-2 (accessed April 22, 2019).
5. Campbell, p. 130.

## CHAPTER 3

## Mexico Goes to War

1. Stephen L. Moore, *Texas Rising: The Epic True Story of the Lone Star Republic and the Rise of the Texas Rangers, 1836–1846* (New York, NY: William Morrow, 2015), p. 36.
2. Richard Bruce Winders, *Sacrificed at the Alamo: Tragedy and Triumph in the Texas Revolution* (Abilene, TX: State House Press, 2004), p. 54.
3. Ben H. Proctor, *The Battle of the Alamo* (Austin, TX: Texas State Historical Association, 1986), p. 1.
4. Proctor, p. 10.
5. Proctor, p. 10.

## CHAPTER 4

## Lesson for the Texians

1. Phillip Thomas Tucker, *Exodus from the Alamo: The Anatomy of the Last Stand Myth* (Philadelphia, PA: Casmate, 2010), pp. 75–76.
2. Walter Lord, *A Time to Stand* (New York, NY: Harper & Row, 1961), p. 101.
3. James Donovan, *The Blood of Heroes: The 13-Day Struggle for the Alamo—And the Sacrifice That Forged a Nation* (New York, NY: Little, Brown and Company, 2012), p. 202.
4. Donovan, pp. 202–203.
5. Donovan, pp. 202–203.
6. Bill Groneman, *Eyewitness to the Alamo* (Lanham, MD: Republic of Texas Press, 2001), p. 7.

## CHAPTER 5

## Besieged!

1. James Donovan, *The Blood of Heroes: The 13-Day Struggle for the Alamo—And the Sacrifice That Forged a Nation* (New York, NY: Little, Brown and Company, 2012), p. 179.
2. William C. Davis, *Three Roads to the Alamo: The Lives and Fortunes of David Crockett, James Bowie, and William Barret Travis* (New York, NY: HarperCollins Publishers, 1998), p. 541.
3. Davis, p. 541.
4. Donovan, p. 242.
5. Davis, pp. 552–553.

## CHAPTER 6

## Victory or Death

1. Bill Groneman, *Eyewitness to the Alamo* (Lanham, MD: Republic of Texas Press, 2001), p. 11.
2. Groneman, pp. 11–12.
3. Groneman, pp. 11–12.
4. Phillip Thomas Tucker, *Exodus from the Alamo: The Anatomy of the Last Stand Myth* (Philadelphia, PA: Casmate, 2010), p. 182.
5. William C. Davis, *Three Roads to the Alamo: The Lives and Fortunes of David Crockett, James Bowie, and William Barret Travis* (New York, NY: HarperCollins Publishers, 1998), pp. 552–553.
6. Stephen L. Moore, *Texas Rising: The Epic True Story of the Lone Star Republic and the Rise of the Texas Rangers, 1836–1846* (New York, NY: William Morrow, 2015), p. 117.
7. Tucker, pp. 263–264.

## CHAPTER 7

## The Bugle Sounds

1. "Deguello," The Handbook of Texas Online, updated September 15, 2015, https://tshaonline.org/handbook/online/articles/xed01.

2. William C. Davis, *Three Roads to the Alamo: The Lives and Fortunes of David Crockett, James Bowie, and William Barret Travis* (New York, NY: HarperCollins Publishers, 1998), p. 560.
3. Davis, p. 560.
4. George J. Dimmick, *Sea of Mud* (Austin, TX: Texas State Historical Association, 2004), p. 109.
5. Timothy M. Matovina, *The Alamo Remembered: Tejano Accounts and Perspectives* (Austin, TX: University of Texas Press, 1995), pp. 84–85.
6. Crystal Sasse Ragdale, *Women and Children of the Alamo* (Austin, TX: State House Press, 1994), p. 60.
7. Dimmick, 116.
8. Matovina, p.53.
9. Matovina, p. 46.
10. Matovina, p. 84.
11. Stephen L. Hardin, "Alamo, Battle of the," The Handbook of Texas Online, updated March 30, 2017, https://tshaonline.org/handbook/online/articles/qea02.

## CHAPTER 8

## San Antonio Reclaimed

1. James Donovan, *The Blood of Heroes: The 13-Day Struggle for the Alamo—And the Sacrifice That Forged a Nation* (New York, NY: Little, Brown and Company, 2012), p. 293.
2. Donovan, p. 293.
3. Gregg J. Dimmick, *Sea of Mud* (Austin, TX: Texas State Historical Association, 2004), p. 126.
4. Dimmick, p. 126.
5. James L. Haley, *Passionate Nation: The Epic History of Texas* (New York, NY: Free Press, 2006, p. 163.
8. Haley, p. 163.
7. Haley, p. 164.
8. Donovan, p. 295.

9. Timothy M. Matovina, *The Alamo Remembered: Tejano Accounts and Perspectives* (Austin, TX: Texas University Press, 1995), p. 44.
10. Dimmick, p. 126.
11. Donovan, p. 348.
12. Davis, p. 567.
13. Davis, p. 568.
14. Davis, p. 568.
15. Dimmick, p. 126.
16. Dimmick, p. 126.

## CHAPTER 9

## The Republic of Texas

1. Gregg J. Dimmick, *Sea of Mud* (Austin, TX: Texas State Historical Association, 2004), p. 126.
2. Dimmick, p. 125.
3. Charles A. Spain Jr., "Flags of Texas," The Handbook of Texas Online, updated July 30, 2018, https://tshaonline.org/handbook/online/articles/msf01.
4. Robert Penn Warren, *Remember the Alamo!* (New York, NY: Random House, 1958), pp. 106–107.
5. "Victory at San Jacinto," San Jacinto Museum of History, https://www.sanjacinto-museum.org/The_Battle/Birth_of_a_Republic (accessed April 22, 2019).
6. Warren, p. 171.
7. James Donovan, *The Blood of Heroes: The 13-Day Struggle for the Alamo—And the Sacrifice That Forged a Nation* (New York, NY: Little, Brown and Company, 2012), p. 332.
8. Randolph B. Campbell, *Gone to Texas: A History of the Lone Star State* (New York, NY: Oxford University Press, 2003), p. 157.
9. Christopher Klein, "6 Things You May Not Know About Santa Anna," History, May 13, 2015, https://www.history.com/news/6-things-you-may-not-know-about-santa-anna.

### CHAPTER 10

## The Twenty-Eighth State Today

1. Randy Roberts and James S. Olsen, *A Line in the Sand* (New York, NY: The Free Press, 2001), p. 155.
2. Roberts and Olsen, p. 175.
3. James E. Crisp, *Sleuthing the Alamo: Davy Crockett's Last Stand and Other Mysteries of the Texas Revolution* (New York, NY: Oxford University Press, 2005), pp. 119–120.
4. Jeff Long, *Duel of Eagles* (New York, NY: William Morrow and Company, 1990), p. 335.
5. "Preservation Work Begins on the Long Barrack," Medium, January 7, 2019, https://medium.com/the-alamo-messenger/preservation-work-begins-on-the-long-barrack-1f324bc8d674.

## Conclusion

1. Phillip Thomas Tucker, *Exodus from the Alamo: The Anatomy of the Last Stand Myth* (Philadelphia, PA: Casmate, 2010), p. 328.
2. Tucker, p. 340.
3. Tucker, p. 323.

# GLOSSARY

**battery** A set of heavy guns or cannon.

**bayou** A small stream.

**carnage** Great and usually bloody slaughter or injury.

***degüello*** The act of beheading or throat-cutting.

**earthwork** An embankment made by piling up dirt, which is used as a fortification.

**garrison** A fortified place with troops.

**grievance** A cause of distress that gives someone reason to complain or resist.

**hardtack** Unleavened bread made into hard, large wafers.

**imperishable** Enduring forever.

**millennia** Thousands of years.

**negotiate** To bring about a compromise through discussion.

**palisade** A fence made of pointed stakes.

**renovation** The restoration to a former better state by cleaning, repairing, or rebuilding.

**secede** To withdraw from an organization.

**skirmish** A minor fight in a war.

**Tejano** A Mexican-born person who lived in Texas.

**Texian** A term that refers to the early settlers of the Texas Territory while it was still under Mexican rule as well as Texas citizens after it gained independence. Today residents of Texas are called Texans.

# FURTHER INFORMATION

## BOOKS

Crockett, David. *Davy Crockett: His Own Story, A Narrative of the Life of Davy Crockett.* Carlisle, MA: Applewood Books, 1993.

Hart, Ken. *It Was a Small Affair.* Pensecola, FL: World Castle Publishing, 2018.

Peppas, Lynn. *The Battle of the Alamo.* New York: Crabtree Publishing, 2017.

Winders, Richard Bruce. *Sacrificed at the Alamo: Tragedy and Triumph in the Texas Revolution.* Abelene, TX: State House Press/McWhiney Foundation, 2018.

Wray, Floyd. *The Battle of the Alamo: A 3D Interactive Adventure in Augmented Reality.* San Antonio, TX: Experience Real History, 2018.

## WEBSITES

**The Alamo**

www.thealamo.org/

*Visit the Alamo digital battlefield and discover events happening at the historic site now.*

**History: The Alamo**

www.history.com/topics/mexico/alamo

*Read more about the Alamo's history, the legendary battle, and its legacy.*

**San Jacinto Museum of History**

www.sanjacinto-museum.org/

*Learn how a decisive eighteen-minute battle for independence changed the course of Texas history.*

## FILMS

*American Experience: Remember the Alamo* (2004), directed by Joseph Tovares.

*The History Channel Presents the Alamo* (2011).

*Wild West Tech: Alamo Tech* (2011), directed by Greystone.

# INDEX

## T



## U



## W



## Z